Functional Skills
English
Level 1

About this book

This book is for anyone doing Level 1 Functional Skills English.
It covers everything you need for the reading and writing parts of the test.

All the topics are explained in a straightforward way, with test-style
questions to give you plenty of useful practice before the final test.

A bit about CGP

Since 1995, CGP study books have helped millions of students do well in
their tests and exams. We cover dozens of subjects for all ages
— and we always keep our prices as low as possible.

Study & Test Practice

Contents

Part 1 — Reading

Section 1 — How Texts Present Ideas

Section 2 — Reading for Detail

Reading Test Practice

Part 2 — Writing

Section 1 — Writing Structure and Planning

Published by CGP

Editors:
Heather Gregson
Anthony Muller
Holly Poynton
Jo Sharrock
Rebecca Tate

With thanks to David Broadbent, Claire Bradshaw and Peter Allen for the proofreading.
With thanks to Laura Collar for the copyright research.

Acknowledgements:
With thanks to iStockphoto.com for permission to use the images on pages 28 and 36
Image on page 34: Ants Tunnelling Through NASA Gel © Copyright Steve Jurvetson, and licensed for reuse under the Creative Commons Licence

All names, places and incidents are fictitious, any resemblance to actual events or persons is entirely coincidental.

ISBN: 978 1 84762 875 6

Printed by Elanders Ltd, Newcastle upon Tyne.
Clipart from Corel®

What is Functional English?

Functional Skills are a set of qualifications

1) They're designed to give you the **skills** you need in **everyday life**.

2) There are **three** Functional Skills **subjects** — **English**, **Maths** and **ICT**.

3) You may have to sit **tests** in **one**, **two** or all **three** of these subjects.

4) Each subject has **five levels** — **Entry Level 1-3**, **Level 1** and **Level 2**.

This book is for Functional English

1) There are **three** parts to English — **speaking and listening**, **reading** and **writing**.

2) To get a Functional Skills English qualification, you need to **pass all three parts**.

3) This book covers the **reading** and **writing** parts of **Functional English Level 1**.

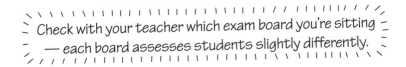

Check with your teacher which exam board you're sitting — each board assesses students slightly differently.

There are two tests and a controlled assessment

For more about controlled assessments check the glossary.

1) **Speaking and listening** is tested by a **controlled assessment** in class.

2) Reading and writing are tested in **two separate tests**.

Reading

- In the **test**, you have to **read two texts** and **answer questions** on both.

- Some questions might be **multiple choice** (you choose the correct answer).

- Some questions might ask you to **write** your **answer**.

- You **don't** have to write in **full sentences**.

- You **won't** lose marks if you make **spelling** or **grammar mistakes**.

Writing

- In the **test**, there are **two questions** you have to **answer**.

- You **will lose marks** if your spelling, grammar and punctuation are **wrong**.

How to Use this Book

This book summarises everything you need to know

1) This book is designed to help you **go over** what you're already learning in class.

2) Use it along with any **notes** and **resources** your teacher has given you.

3) You can work through this book from **start** to **finish**...

4) ...or you can just **pick the topics** that you're **not sure** about.

Use this book to revise and test yourself

1) This book is split into **two parts** — **reading** and **writing**.

2) The topics in each part are usually **spread over two pages**:

Here's the title of the topic.

On the left-hand page there's all the important information for each topic.

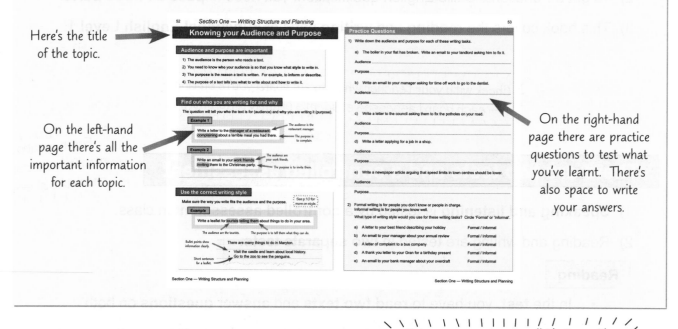

On the right-hand page there are practice questions to test what you've learnt. There's also space to write your answers.

There are answers to all the practice questions and the test-style exercises at the end of each part of the book.

There's lots of test-style practice

1) There are **test-style practice exercises** at the **end** of each part of the book.

2) These exercises are based on **actual Functional English assessments**.

3) This means that the questions are **similar** to the ones you'll be asked in the **real tests**.

4) The **reading tests** have a **mix** of **question types** with **space** to write your answers.

5) The **writing tests** have space for a **plan**, but you'll need **extra paper** for your full answer.

Using a Dictionary

You can use a dictionary in the test

1) You can use a dictionary to look up the **meaning** of a tricky word.

2) Or you can look up a word to check its **spelling**.

Here's the word you're looking up.

This is one meaning of the word.

qualm (kwa:m) *n* **1** a feeling of sickness **2** a feeling of doubt

This is how you say the word.

This is another meaning.

Practise using a dictionary before the test

1) The words in a **dictionary** are listed in **alphabetical order**.

2) This means all the words starting with '**a**' are **grouped together** first, then all the words starting with '**b**', and so on.

3) Each **letter** in a word is also listed in **alphabetical order**.

4) When you're looking up a word, check the words in **bold** at the **top** of **each page**.

5) These words help you work out which **page** you need to **turn to**.

This tells you that all the words between 'rush' and 'rustle' are covered on this page.

If you want a word that comes before 'rush', turn to an earlier page. If you want a word that comes after 'rustle', turn to a later page.

This is the page number of the dictionary.

984   **rush | rustle**

rush *vb* **1** to hurry

The first letter that is different for these words is the fourth letter. 'h' comes before 't' in the alphabet, so 'rush' comes before 'rustle'.

Don't use a dictionary all the time

1) Dictionaries can be **helpful**, but **don't** use them **too often**.

2) Looking up **lots** of words will **slow you down** in the test...

3) ...so try to **learn** the **spelling** of **tricky** words **before the test**.

If there's a word you don't recognise in this book, use a dictionary to look it up. It's a good way of practising.

Test Advice

Use this general advice for your tests

1) **Read** and **understand** what each question **wants you to do** before answering it.

2) Write **clearly** or you could **lose marks**. If you make a mistake just correct it **neatly**.

3) Use your **time sensibly**:

   - Leave enough time to do **all the questions**.
   - Spend **longer** on questions that are worth **more marks**.
   - Spend a few minutes **checking** through your work at the end.

Read the sources carefully in the Reading Test

1) Read the **whole text** before you answer any questions.

2) Make sure you only pick out **relevant information**.

3) In the **reading test** you **don't** have to use **full sentences**...

4) ...and you **don't** get marks for **spelling**, **punctuation** or **grammar**.

5) If you can't do a question, **leave it** and **move on** to the next one.

6) You can **come back** to the questions you have left if you have time at the end.

Multiple-choice questions

If you're stuck on a **multiple-choice question** make a **sensible guess**.

Written questions

Make sure **each point** you write is **different** and you haven't put the **same thing twice**. Don't write more than you need to because you **won't** get any **extra marks**. For example:

> 7) Using the information in **Source B**, write down **four** examples of how you could help protect the environment.
>
> ....
>
> ....
>
> (4 marks)

Don't write more than four different points because you won't get any extra marks.

Test Advice

Planning is important in the Writing Test

1) Writing a **plan** will help you get your ideas in the **right order**.

2) If you're given **bullet points**, make sure you use them in your plan.

Example

You held your friend's birthday party at a local hotel and everyone really enjoyed it. Write a letter thanking the manager for a great time.

You should include:

It might be helpful to write about the bullet points in the order they are given.

• Why you are writing

• The details of the party

• Why you had such a great time

Your answer should include all these things.

3) You will get marks if your answer has a **clear beginning**, **middle** and **end**.

4) **Don't** spend **too long** on your plan or your draft.

5) Leave enough time to write your **final copy**.

Write clearly and correctly in the Writing Test

1) Use **full sentences** and **paragraphs** to make your writing clear.

2) **Spelling**, **punctuation** and **grammar** are worth a lot of marks.
   Make sure you check for **obvious mistakes**.

3) If you're **copying** a word that's used in a source, make sure you spell it **correctly**.

4) Your **style** and **content** are **important**:

   • **Don't** use **text language** like 'coz' or 'tho', even if you're writing to a friend.

   • Always be **polite**. Even if you are writing to complain, **don't be rude**.

   • If you **make up any details**, be **sensible** and make sure they add something **useful**.

   • Use any **similar experiences** you've had to make your writing more **believable**.

The Purposes of Different Texts

Texts have different purposes

1) There are **four** main kinds of text you could come across:
   - **informative** — for example, an article about craft workshops
   - **descriptive** — for example, a review of a holiday camp
   - **instructive** — for example, a recipe for cupcakes
   - **persuasive** — for example, an advert for new trainers

2) Each kind of text has a different **purpose**.

Informative writing tells you about something

1) Informative texts give the reader lots of **information**.

2) They are full of **facts**. **Facts** are statements that can be proved to be **true** or **false**.

Example

The Mini first went on sale in 1959. It soon became the best selling car in Europe. Over five million of them were made and many famous people, including 'The Beatles', bought them.

This example contains lots of facts like dates.

Instructive writing tells you how to do something

1) Instructive texts give the reader **instructions** to follow.

2) They are usually split up into **numbered lists** or **bullet points**.

3) They use **clear language** to make them easy to understand.

See p.13 for more on numbered lists and bullet points.

Example

- If you hear the fire alarm, stop what you are doing.
- Make your way safely to the nearest exit.
- Leave all of your belongings behind.

Simple language makes instructions straightforward.

Each instruction has a separate bullet point.

Practice Questions

Read the text below, and then answer the questions underneath.

Shopping Company Creates New Jobs

It was announced yesterday that the home shopping company Goldson's Total Merchandise (GTM) is to open a new branch in Harsham. The company will open its new site on St. Peters Road in August 2013. It will employ 150 staff to run a brand new call centre and warehouse.

GTM's Managing Director, Lucy Nuttley, said, "We are delighted to have finally tied up the loose ends on this arrangement. This is an exciting development for us as a company and for the Harsham area."

Building work on the site will start immediately. GTM plans to refurbish the offices that already exist on the site, but an entirely new warehouse will be built.

GTM was founded in 2002. It quickly grew to be one of the leading home shopping companies in the UK, with offices in London, Birmingham and Newport.

1) What kind of business is Goldson's Total Merchandise? Circle your answer.

   a)   An internet shopping company   c)   A building company

   b)   A home shopping company   d)   An office supplies company

2) When was Goldson's Total Merchandise founded? Circle your answer.

   a)   2002   c)   2008

   b)   2013   d)   2004

3) Name **one** place where GTM already has offices.

....

4) a)   Is this text informative or instructive? ....

   b)   How can you tell? ....

....

The Purposes of Different Texts

Persuasive writing tries to convince the reader

1) Persuasive texts might use **language** that makes the reader **feel** a certain way.

Example 1

The traffic situation in Little Urswell is a disgrace. Our children are put in danger every day, but the council refuse to do anything. Before long there's going to be a tragedy.

Words like 'disgrace', 'danger' and 'tragedy' make the reader feel angry.

2) They sometimes use **facts** to persuade the reader.

Example 2

Temperatures across the world have increased by about 1°C in the last hundred years. Governments must act to fight climate change because scientists predict that temperatures will continue to rise.

Facts make writing more believable. The writer sounds like an expert.

Descriptive writing tells readers what something is like

1) It uses **describing words** like 'dusty', 'exciting' and 'silently'.

Example 1

The walk begins in a stunning location by a peaceful lake, not far from Yorley Wood. As you wander past the lake, you might see beautiful swans. The route is short but quite steep.

Describing words tell you what the walk is like.

2) Descriptive writing can also **persuade** people.

Example 2

Don't watch this terrible film. Its shallow characters aren't realistic, and their lives were so dull that I fell asleep.

These describing words persuade the reader not to watch the film.

Practice Questions

Read the text below, and then answer the questions underneath.

The coming bank holiday weekend sees Sponfield's ever popular music festival back in Ruskon Park once again. This year's highlights include some old favourites and plenty of new acts as well:

Saturday — THE SOUL SENSATIONS
All the way from Chicago, the Sensations cover all your favourite Motown tunes.

Join us between 10 am and midnight!

Sunday — HELL'S SCORPIONS
These German rockers are returning to give an unmissable heavy metal performance.

Monday — THE MORLEY ORCHESTRA
This world-famous orchestra will impress fans of classical music.

With over thirty acts from all over the world, introduced by superstar DJ Daz Darley, this is a treat not to be missed!

1) The acts performing at the festival are:

   a) All American

   b) All from London

   c) Mostly from the local area

   d) From lots of different countries

2) How many acts are playing at the festival? Circle your answer.

   a) Three

   b) Ten

   c) Over thirty

   d) Less than twelve

3) How many days does the music festival last?

....

4) Your friend wants to see some classical music. What day should she go to the festival?

....

5) a) Is this text descriptive or persuasive? ....

   b) How can you tell? ....

....

Identifying Tone and Style

Writing can have a personal or impersonal tone

1) **Personal** writing sounds like it's **talking to the reader**.

2) It's written from the writer's **point of view**, so it's full of **opinions** and it shows **emotion**.

Example

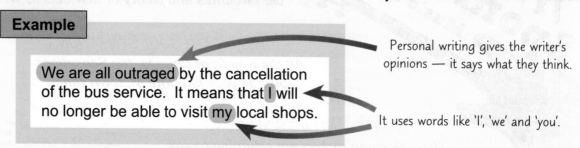

We are all outraged by the cancellation of the bus service. It means that I will no longer be able to visit my local shops.

Personal writing gives the writer's opinions — it says what they think.

It uses words like 'I', 'we' and 'you'.

3) **Impersonal** writing **doesn't** tell you anything about the writer's **personality**.

4) It just reports the **facts**, so it's usually **neutral** and doesn't take anybody's **side**.

Example

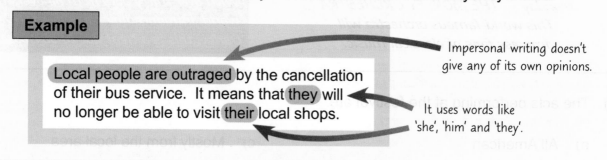

Local people are outraged by the cancellation of their bus service. It means that they will no longer be able to visit their local shops.

Impersonal writing doesn't give any of its own opinions.

It uses words like 'she', 'him' and 'they'.

Writing can have a formal or informal style

1) **Formal** writing sounds **serious**. It usually has an **impersonal tone**.

2) It's used for things like **job applications** because it **sounds** more **professional**.

Example

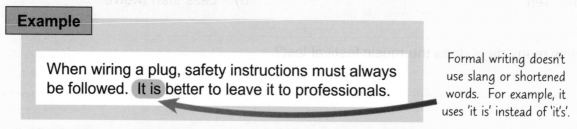

When wiring a plug, safety instructions must always be followed. It is better to leave it to professionals.

Formal writing doesn't use slang or shortened words. For example, it uses 'it is' instead of 'it's'.

3) **Informal** writing sounds **chatty**. It usually has a **personal tone**.

4) It's used for things like **letters** to your **family** because it's more **friendly**.

Example

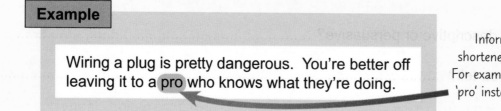

Wiring a plug is pretty dangerous. You're better off leaving it to a pro who knows what they're doing.

Informal writing uses shortened words and slang. For example, it uses the slang 'pro' instead of 'professional'.

Practice Questions

Read the text below, and then answer the questions underneath.

From: customerservices@electigen.co.uk

To: e.l.grant@email.co.uk

Send

Subject: RE: Powercuts at 25 Market Street

Dear Mr. Grant,

I am sorry to hear that you are unhappy with the treatment you have received from Electigen Power Services. We are proud of our customer service and we are disappointed that you feel we have not treated you well.

I would like to offer you a free month of electricity to apologise for the numerous power cuts you have suffered. This month of free electricity will begin on the 12th August and will end on the 11th September. I hope this will convince you not to change energy supplier.

Please let us know if you experience any other problems with your electricity.

Warm regards,

Reginald Sprint
Customer Services Manager

---

1) a) Is the tone of this email personal or impersonal? ....

   b) How can you tell?

   ....

   ....

2) Why do you think this tone has been used? Circle your answer.

   a) It sounds more professional   c) To show that Mr Grant is wrong

   b) The writer is friends with Mr Grant   d) To show that the writer cares

3) a) Is the style of this email formal or informal? ....

   b) How can you tell?

   ....

   ....

4) Why do you think this style has been used?

   a) It sounds more business-like   c) To seem friendly and kind

   b) The writer is angry   d) To give information clearly

Recognising How a Text is Presented

Presentational features help the reader understand the text

1) Some texts use things like **headings**, **bullet points** and **colour**.

2) These are called **presentational features**, **layout features** or **organisational devices**.

3) They help make the text **easier to understand**, and make its **purpose clearer**.

Headlines tell you what an article is about

1) They are always **bigger** than all the other words and are at the **top** of the page.

2) They try to **grab** the reader's **attention** and get them to read the article.

3) The **tone** of the headline can give you a clue about the **mood** of the **article**.

Example 1

Four Die in Brighton House Fire

This headline is serious. It tells you what the article is about.

Example 2

Electric Cars Spark Sales

This headline is humorous. 'Spark' could mean a spark of electricity or something that starts off the sales.

Subheadings and columns break up text

Newspapers and leaflets use **columns** and **subheadings** to make things **clear**.

Example

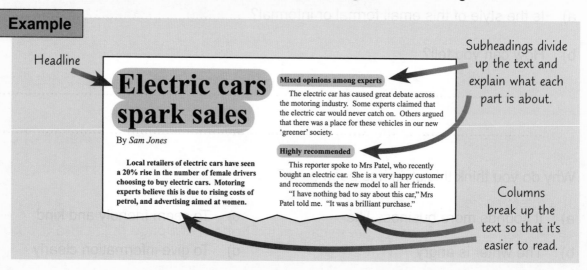

Headline →

Electric cars spark sales

By *Sam Jones*

Local retailers of electric cars have seen a 20% rise in the number of female drivers choosing to buy electric cars. Motoring experts believe this is due to rising costs of petrol, and advertising aimed at women.

Mixed opinions among experts

The electric car has caused great debate across the motoring industry. Some experts claimed that the electric car would never catch on. Others argued that there was a place for these vehicles in our new 'greener' society.

Highly recommended

This reporter spoke to Mrs Patel, who recently bought an electric car. She is a very happy customer and recommends the new model to all her friends. "I have nothing bad to say about this car," Mrs Patel told me. "It was a brilliant purchase."

Subheadings divide up the text and explain what each part is about.

Columns break up the text so that it's easier to read.

Section One — How Texts Present Ideas

Recognising How a Text is Presented

Paragraphs divide text up into chunks

1) When writers introduce a **new subject** or **idea**, they start a **new paragraph**.

2) This helps give their writing a **structure** and makes it easier to **understand**.

Example

Caroline, the main character, is the best thing about this book. By the end she almost feels like a friend.

However, the book is let down by its plot. It is so ridiculous that it could have been thought up by a child.

A new paragraph starts here. This shows where the part about Caroline ends and the part about the plot begins.

Bullet points and numbered lists divide up texts

1) **Bullet points** separate information into **short** bits of text so it's **easier** to **read**.

Example

Bullet points separate each piece of information. This makes the writing clear.

If you have a complaint, please contact us by:
- Emailing us at complaints@tigerjewels.com
- Telephoning us on 01222 333 444

2) **Numbered lists** can be used instead of bullet points.

3) This is usually for things that are **in an order**, like a set of **instructions**.

See p.113-114 for an example glossary.

References and glossaries give extra information

1) If a writer has used information from **other sources** they might say **where** they got it from.

2) This is called **referencing**. **References** say **where** the information is from and **who** it's by.

3) Writers sometimes **explain** difficult words in a **glossary**.

4) Glossaries and references are usually at the **bottom** of a **page** or the **end** of a **book**.

Recognising How a Text is Presented

Graphics and captions help you understand a text

A **graphic** is a **picture**, **diagram** or **chart**. It gives you **extra information** about the text.

Example

Can Graffiti Ever Be Considered Art?

Graffiti has been around for many years, and it is usually dismissed as simple vandalism. However, in recent months there has been growing pressure from the art community to recognise it as its own art form.

Graffiti on a wall in Brixton

The graphic shows the type of graffiti the text is talking about.

A caption is a bit of text that tells you more about the graphic.

Colour affects how you read a text

1) The **colour** of a **text**, or its **background**, creates an effect on the reader.

2) **Bright colours** make text look more **fun**.

3) **Dark colours** create a **serious mood** suitable for more **formal** texts.

Fonts help set the tone of a text

1) A text's **font** gives you a clue about what **kind** of text it is.

2) **Serious, formal** fonts are for **serious, formal** texts.

3) **Cartoony, childish** fonts are for **light-hearted** texts or texts for **children**.

Example

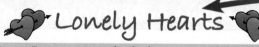

Ben, 23 — Lancaster lad, born and bred. Looking for a girl of similar age who enjoys cycling.

Amy, 32 — Young-at-heart clubber seeks man aged 26-40 in London area to party the night away with.

The colour red is connected with love. The handwriting font makes it seem more personal.

The bold font helps divide the text up.

Practice Questions

Read the text below, and then answer the questions underneath.

Children's Party Games
by Jesse Gallagher

Port and Starboard

Read a command from the list on the right (or any command of your own), and tell the children to do the appropriate action. After a while, start removing the last child to do the action, until only one is left. This child is the winner.

Pass the Parcel

Wrap a present in about 10 layers of wrapping paper. (You could put sweets or forfeits between the layers if you fancy.) Play some music. Everyone sits in a circle and passes the parcel from one person to the next. When the music stops, the person holding the parcel removes ONE layer of wrapping. Repeat until the last layer has been removed. The winner keeps the present.

Commands

- **Port** (Run to the left side of the room)
- **Starboard** (Run to the right side)
- **Submarines** (Lie on the floor)
- **Climb the rigging** (Run on the spot)
- **Mess deck** (Sit on the floor)
- **Up periscope** (Hands in the air)

1) The **main** purpose of this text is to:

   a) Tell children how to have fun

   b) Teach the rules of 'Port and Starboard'

   c) Describe how to throw a kid's party

   d) Give ideas for party games to play

2) Give **one** presentational feature that shows that the article is light-hearted.

   ....

3) List **two** ways the article has been presented and say
   why it helps the reader understand the article better.

   a) Presentational feature: ....

      This helps reader understanding because: ....

      ....

   b) Presentational feature: ....

      This helps reader understanding because: ....

      ....

Spotting Different Types of Text

Letters and emails have standard layouts

1) Letters have an **address**, the **date** and a **greeting** at the top, with a **sign-off** at the bottom.

2) Emails have a '**to**' and a '**from**' box at the top, as well as a box for the email's **subject**.

See p.64 for an example letter. See p.66 for an example email.

Adverts and leaflets try to grab your attention

1) Adverts are **persuasive**. They try to **convince** you to do something.

2) Leaflets are **informative**. They give you **information** about something.

3) Adverts and leaflets both use **colours**, **pictures** and different **fonts** to get **noticed**.

Example

Carnaby Castle Tours

Carnaby Castle is the **smallest** castle in the UK! Take a tour of this tiny castle and see what life was **really** like for the people who lived there **hundreds** of years ago.

- Tours run every hour
- Open 10 am to 4 pm
- Prices: £5.00 for adults
  £3.00 for children

An interesting font and logo grab the reader's attention.

Colour makes the leaflet look attractive.

Bullet points keep information simple and easy to read.

Websites have specific features

They usually have an **address bar** at the top, a **search box** and **links** to other **webpages**.

Example

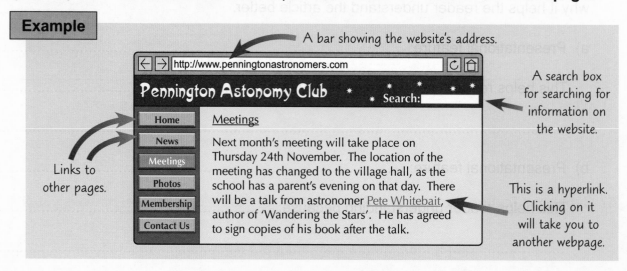

A bar showing the website's address.

http://www.penningtonastronomers.com

Pennington Astonomy Club   Search:

| Home |
| News |
| Meetings |
| Photos |
| Membership |
| Contact Us |

Meetings

Next month's meeting will take place on Thursday 24th November. The location of the meeting has changed to the village hall, as the school has a parent's evening on that day. There will be a talk from astronomer Pete Whitebait, author of 'Wandering the Stars'. He has agreed to sign copies of his book after the talk.

A search box for searching for information on the website.

Links to other pages.

This is a hyperlink. Clicking on it will take you to another webpage.

Spotting Different Types of Text

Articles are in newspapers or magazines

See p.12 for an example article.

1) They have **headlines** to tell you what the article is **about**.

2) **Subheadings** and **columns** are used to break up the text.

Practice Questions

Look at the four text types below and then answer the questions underneath each one.

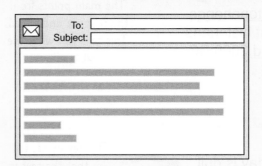

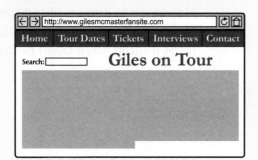

1) What type of text is this?

....

2) Name **one** feature that tells you this.

....

3) What type of text is this?

....

4) Name **one** feature that tells you this.

....

5) What type of text is this?

....

6) Name **one** feature that tells you this.

....

7) What type of text is this?

....

8) Name **one** feature that tells you this.

....

Picking Out the Main Points

Skim the text to work out the main points

1) You **don't** need to read **all** of a text to find the **main points**.

2) Move your eyes **quickly** over the text, looking for **key words**.

3) **Key words** are things that tell you **who**, **what**, **where**, **when**, **why** and **how**.

4) **Underline** any key words that you find.

Example 1

Not much is known about the <u>origins of Stonehenge</u>. <u>Nobody knows when</u> it was built, but most historians think it must have been between <u>3000 and 2000 BC</u>.

The main points from the text are underlined. This tells you what the text is about.

Example 2

Staying inside watching television every day is <u>dull</u> and <u>unhealthy</u>. There are many <u>exciting</u> and <u>healthy</u> outdoor activities that are available in the area, like jogging, sports teams and rowing. <u>Get involved</u>!

The key words tell you that the text is trying to persuade people to do outdoor activities.

The most important point usually comes first

1) Each **paragraph** in a text has its **own main point**.

2) The **most important point** is usually in the **first paragraph**.

Example

12 Lower Brook Street, Sanditon

This is a newly-decorated detached house in a fantastic area on the outskirts of Sanditon. Its location is quiet and rural, but still within easy reach of the town centre.

The property has four bedrooms, a lounge, a fitted kitchen, a dining room and two bathrooms.

The location of the house is the most important point. It's in the first paragraph.

The second paragraph gives extra details.

Practice Questions

Read the text below, and then answer the questions underneath.

 **Annette Bakes**

Search: [＿＿＿＿＿]

| Home | Shops | Cakes | Recipes | Awards | FAQs | Contact |

Annette Grey
Managing Director

Frequently Asked Questions

How did you get into baking? I've loved baking since I was a child. One of my earliest memories is of adding flour to a cake mixture with the bowl balanced on a stool. I was in my grandmother's kitchen and it went absolutely everywhere! I must have been about five.

How did you turn your hobby into a business? I left school at 17, when I got pregnant, and I didn't really know what to do. I started baking cakes for my daughter's birthday parties. Soon the other mothers were paying me to bake for their kids too. I guess it was an accident, really.

What would you do if you weren't a baker? I always wanted to be in the fire service. I really admire the incredible courage of firefighters.

1) Name **one** presentational feature that tells you this is a website.

....

2) What is the **main** point of this text? Circle your answer.

   a) To describe Annette's bakery   c) To tell people how to start a business

   b) To tell the reader about Annette's life   d) To convince people to become firefighters

3) How did Annette get into baking? Circle your answer.

   a) She couldn't be a firefighter   c) She hated school

   b) Her grandmother ran a bakery   d) She baked cakes for children's birthdays

4) How old was Annette when she left school?

....

5) Why has Annette always wanted to be in the fire service?

....

Using Layout to Help

The layout of a text can help you find details

1) **Layout features**, like subheadings, tell you **where** different information is.

2) Use them to decide which **part** of a text to **check first**.

3) Then **scan** this part of the text to find the **details** you're looking for.

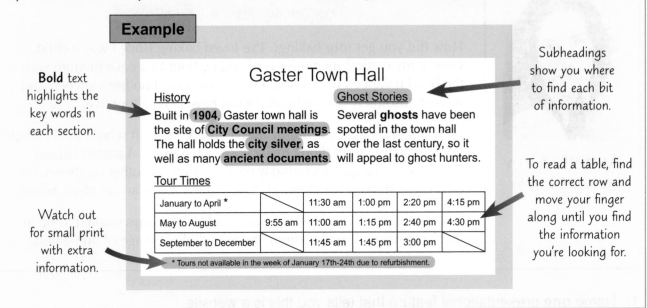

Example

Bold text highlights the key words in each section.

Subheadings show you where to find each bit of information.

Watch out for small print with extra information.

To read a table, find the correct row and move your finger along until you find the information you're looking for.

Gaster Town Hall

History
Built in **1904**, Gaster town hall is the site of **City Council meetings**. The hall holds the **city silver**, as well as many **ancient documents**.

Ghost Stories
Several **ghosts** have been spotted in the town hall over the last century, so it will appeal to ghost hunters.

Tour Times

January to April *		11:30 am	1:00 pm	2:20 pm	4:15 pm
May to August	9:55 am	11:00 am	1:15 pm	2:40 pm	4:30 pm
September to December		11:45 am	1:45 pm	3:00 pm	

* Tours not available in the week of January 17th-24th due to refurbishment.

Look for key words in the text

Use the **question** to help you find the information you need.

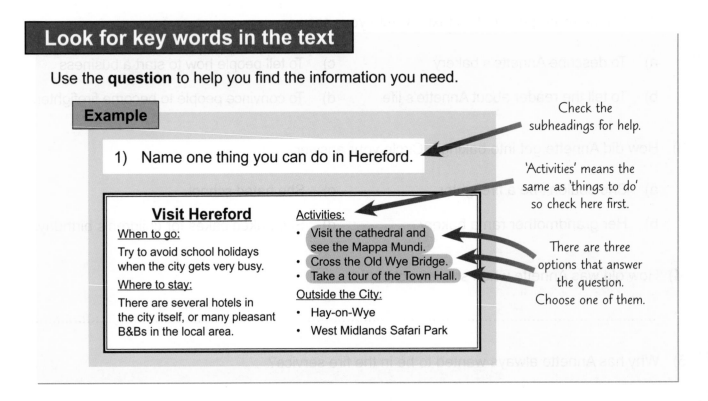

Example

Check the subheadings for help.

'Activities' means the same as 'things to do' so check here first.

There are three options that answer the question. Choose one of them.

1) Name one thing you can do in Hereford.

Visit Hereford

When to go:
Try to avoid school holidays when the city gets very busy.

Where to stay:
There are several hotels in the city itself, or many pleasant B&Bs in the local area.

Activities:
- Visit the cathedral and see the Mappa Mundi.
- Cross the Old Wye Bridge.
- Take a tour of the Town Hall.

Outside the City:
- Hay-on-Wye
- West Midlands Safari Park

Practice Questions

Read the text below, and then answer the questions underneath.

Weather Forecast — Wednesday 23rd April

Scotland & Northern England
Warm, dry and sunny conditions for the whole day.

Northern Ireland
Low clouds with outbreaks of drizzly rain. Coastal areas may experience mist and fog patches.

Wales & South West England
Low clouds, with showers likely later in the day.

Southern England & Midlands
Overcast with sunny intervals throughout the morning. Clouds will clear later in the day.

Temperature chart

Temperature (ºC)	6 am-10 am	10 am-2 pm	2 pm-6 pm
Scotland & Northern England	13	17	16
Northern Ireland	13	16	17
Wales & South West England	12	14	14
Southern England & Midlands	15	19	18

The rest of the week
Sunny intervals over most of the country, with warm showers likely in western areas on Friday. Strong winds in the south west and north.

1) What temperature will it be in Northern Ireland at 11 am? Circle your answer.

   a) 16 ºC

   b) 13 ºC

   c) 14 ºC

   d) 19 ºC

2) What will the weather be like in the Midlands in the morning? Circle your answer.

   a) Showers and low clouds

   b) Warm, dry and sunny conditions

   c) Overcast with sunny intervals

   d) Cloudy but clearing

3) Where are warm showers likely on Friday?

   ....

4) Which area will have the highest temperature at 5 pm?

   ....

5) What areas of Northern Ireland might see patches of fog?

   ....

Answering Tricky Questions

Some questions ask you to understand information

Harder questions might ask you to **use** facts, not just **find** them.

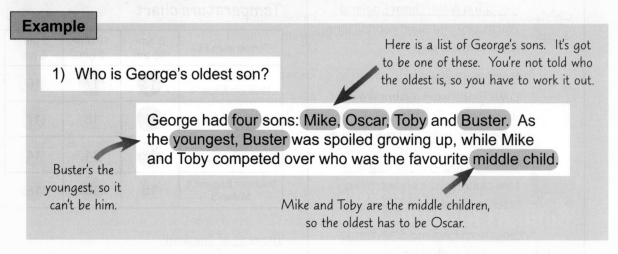

Example

1) Who is George's oldest son?

Here is a list of George's sons. It's got to be one of these. You're not told who the oldest is, so you have to work it out.

George had four sons: Mike, Oscar, Toby and Buster. As the youngest, Buster was spoiled growing up, while Mike and Toby competed over who was the favourite middle child.

Buster's the youngest, so it can't be him.

Mike and Toby are the middle children, so the oldest has to be Oscar.

The answer might be unclear for multiple-choice questions

1) In multiple-choice questions you'll be given a **right** answer and some **wrong** ones.

2) Some **wrong** answers might **sound right**.

3) **Rule out** the **options** that are **definitely wrong** until you're left with the **right answer**.

Example

Soup is an easy and healthy dish to cook. Just take your favourite vegetables (for example, beans, carrots, potatoes or broccoli) and boil them until soft. Then mash or blend them to make a liquid. Add stock or water and season.

1) What is the main point of this text?
   a) To tell people how to eat healthily
   b) To make people eat more vegetables
   c) To explain the writer's favourite dish
   d) To tell people how to make soup

It mentions that soup is healthy, but this isn't the main point.

It gives examples of vegetables, but doesn't tell people to eat more of them.

The writer's favourite dish isn't mentioned.

This is the right answer. The text is mainly about how to make soup.

Practice Questions

Read the text below, and then answer the questions underneath.

Travelling Hero Returns

Joseph Redman has been racing in his wheelchair for the last five years, but his latest challenge was a bit different. Instead of competing in a race against other wheelchair users, he has wheeled himself from Land's End to John O'Groats. So far he has raised more than £5000 for charity.

Redman set off on Tuesday 1st October, after a year of tough training. He arrived at his first checkpoint five days later, suffering from a cold. This slowed him down for the rest of his challenge, and he finally finished on Thursday 24th after eighteen more days — six days later than he'd planned.

Support Joseph!

Donate at:

www.josephredman.com

After a rest, Joseph said he was thrilled with his performance.

"Climbing the hills was tough, but going downhill I could just let myself roll all the way. You can't do that if you're running!"

If you'd like to watch Joseph's video diary, go to our website, www.rainhamtimes.com, and follow the links. If you'd like to donate to Joseph's chosen charities, please visit his website.

1) What day of the week did Joseph arrive at his first checkpoint? Circle your answer.

   a) Friday   c) Saturday

   b) Sunday   d) Tuesday

2) What is the **main** point of this article? Circle your answer.

   a) To tell people about Joseph's challenge   c) To advertise Joseph's charity

   b) To persuade people to visit Land's End   d) To tell people about wheelchairs

3) How many days late did Joseph arrive at his destination? Circle your answer.

   a) 18   c) 6

   b) 5   d) 24

4) What should you do if you want to watch a video about his challenge? Circle your answer.

   a) Go to Joseph's website   c) Go to www.rainhamtimes.com

   b) Look out for it on the news   d) Visit the charity's website

Answering Tricky Questions

Some questions ask about a text's purpose

You have to read **all** of a text carefully to work out its **purpose**.

Example

> The car was travelling quickly along the road when a cyclist rode out from a driveway a few metres in front of it. He had a bright red bike and was wearing reflective clothes, with a green helmet. The car had to swerve off the road to avoid the cyclist. It hit a tree and was damaged. The cyclist rode off.

1) What is the purpose of this text?

   a) To persuade the police to arrest the cyclist

   b) To complain about the speed limit

   c) To describe a road accident

   d) To persuade cyclists to wear helmets

It doesn't give any opinions about whether the cyclist should be arrested.

It doesn't say that the speed limit is too fast or too slow.

It gives a description of what made the car crash into the tree. This is the right answer.

It only mentions the green helmet the cyclist was wearing.

Pick information carefully when you write your own answer

1) **Read** each question **carefully** and work out what information **fits** best.

2) You might have to **ignore** a lot of information.

3) Look at the **number of marks**. **Write one thing** for each mark.

For the reading test, you don't have to write in full sentences.

Example

1) What does the report suggest that the council should do?

> The recent accident on Greenley Road was caused by a driver going too fast along the road. The cyclist's driveway is hidden from the road, so the driver did not know to slow down. The cyclist should have looked before exiting.
>
> To prevent another accident like this, the council should build speed bumps along this road. The owner of the driveway should also put up a mirror so he can see the road when he pulls out of his drive.

The first paragraph is about what caused the accident. You can ignore it.

This sentence tells you what the council should do. This is the answer.

The last sentence is about what the driveway's owner should do, so you can ignore it as well.

Practice Questions

Read the text below, and then answer the questions underneath.

reliablehotelreviews.com

Hotels in Mifton

Mifton Villa Hotel

☆★★★★★

Don't make the same mistake I did. Avoid this hotel. Overpriced rooms, unfriendly staff, portions of food just big enough for a mouse... And worst of all — absolutely nothing to do. An expensive weekend of total boredom.

Snapdragon B&B

☆☆☆☆☆

I can't recommend this hotel highly enough! The staff were polite and helpful, and the rooms were clean and cosy. It's the perfect getaway for people just wanting to relax in the lounge and read a good book in peace.

Sandpiper Cottage

☆☆☆☆★

A beautiful building right next to a large park. The rooms are spacious and the hotel has a swimming pool with water slides. The staff are very friendly, although I felt that the portions at breakfast could have been a bit more generous.

1) What is the **main** purpose of the webpage? Circle your answer.

   a)   To persuade people to stay in hotels

   b)   To tell people about Mifton

   c)   To help people choose a hotel

   d)   To recommend Snapdragon B&B

2) What is the **main** purpose of the Mifton Villa Hotel review? Circle your answer.

   a)   To persuade people not to stay there

   b)   To tell people about activities in Mifton

   c)   To describe the hotel

   d)   To recommend the hotel to others

3) Your friend is worried that her children will get bored while they are away in Mifton.

   a)   Which hotel would you suggest they stay at?

   ....

   b)   Give **two** reasons for your answer.

   1. ....

   ....

   2. ....

   ....

Section Two — Reading for Detail

Source A — Second-Hand Cars

Read **Source A** and answer the questions that follow. You have 15 minutes to do this exercise.

For multiple-choice questions, circle the letter you have chosen.
For standard answer questions, write your answer in the space provided.
You do not have to write in full sentences. You may use a dictionary.

SAM FAST MOTORS

Are you looking for a great deal on a used car?

Want a fair price for your part-exchange?

We have the biggest range of used cars in East London. Whatever you're after, we can offer you the best value deal you'll find anywhere.

At Sam Fast Motors, our staff are trained to be informed, helpful and polite — with none of the pushiness you get with other dealerships.

All our cars have been carefully tested, so you can be confident your car will be safe and reliable. You'll have years of happy motoring ahead.

Our one year warranty comes standard with any purchase. If you do have any issues, you'll be covered by our 'no fuss guarantee'.

So why not pop in for a friendly chat with one of our sales people and see what we can offer?

TESTIMONIALS

The service was excellent, and I came home with a car that I absolutely love! — J. Anderson

Great selection, great prices. I wouldn't recommend going anywhere else... — Emma Rose

"At Sam Fast Motors, customer satisfaction isn't everything, it's the only thing" — Sam Fast

HOME

ABOUT US

USED CARS

USED BIKES

USED VANS

FAQs

CONTACT US

Sam Fast
Sam Fast MD

Tel: 08098 564222

Fax: 08098 564333

Email:
Info@SFMotors.com

Search for a used car:

Make: Any make

Model: Any model

Looking for cheap car insurance?

Bear Cover

Click here for more details.

Enter your email to join our mailing list:

Example@email.co.uk

JOIN NOW ▶

1) The **main** purpose of the webpage is to:

a) Tell you about the company's history

b) Encourage you to buy a car from them

c) Persuade you to get car insurance

d) Give you their contact details

(1 mark)

2) Which of these statements about the staff at Sam Fast Motors is false:

a)   They all live in East London

c)   They are well-informed

b)   They are friendly

d)   They are helpful and polite

(1 mark)

3) The **main** point of having testimonials is to:

a)   Show you that they have customers

c)   Prove they have satisfied customers

b)   Persuade you to write your own

d)   Fill up space on the website

(1 mark)

4) The webpage informs you that:

a)   You can test drive the cars

c)   They are based in East London

b)   They offer a two year warranty

d)   They don't do part-exchanges

(1 mark)

5) Identify **two** presentational features that show you that Source A is a webpage:

a)   ....

....

b)   ....

....

(2 marks)

6) List **two** reasons why you might buy a used car from Sam Fast Motors:

a)   ....

....

b)   ....

....

(2 marks)

Source B — The GI Diet

Read **Source B** and answer the questions that follow. You have 15 minutes to do this exercise.

For multiple-choice questions, circle the letter you have chosen.
For standard answer questions, write your answer in the space provided.
You do not have to write in full sentences. You may use a dictionary.

You are interested in learning more about nutrition and read this article in a local newspaper.

New Diet Praised by Doctors

BY LUCY TONGE
Lifestyle editor

DESPERATE dieters up and down the country have welcomed reports of a new eating plan which is both healthy and effective. Doctors released the results of their research yesterday, and they believe their findings could lead to a new diet craze sweeping the nation.

Doctors recommend low-sugar foods

Doctors identified whether certain foods had a high or low glycaemic index (GI). The GI tells you how much sugar a food contains. Doctors

■ **FOOD FOR THOUGHT:**
Doctors release new findings

suggested that dieters replace high GI foods, such as potatoes and white bread, with low GI foods like eggs, milk and lean meat. They advised replacing just one high GI item per meal with a low GI item. This can significantly help lower blood sugar levels.

Lower blood sugar levels are important for reducing the risk of heart disease and diabetes.

It is predicted that the diet will be extremely popular, mainly because of its simplicity.

A spokeswoman for Diabetes Concern said the low GI diet was the only one the charity recommended. "It's a good way of controlling blood sugar levels, but it should form part of a balanced diet."

Not a quick-fix

However, the British Nutrition Association (BNA) warned against over-relying on such diets. They pointed out that ice-cream has a low GI value, but eating ice-cream with every meal won't help dieters lose weight. The key to losing weight, they said, is cutting down on calories, eating sensible portions and taking regular exercise.

Low GI foods
apples, fish, pasta, tomatoes, cheese, brown bread, milk

High GI foods
chips, parsnips, white bread, potatoes, white rice

1) The **main** purpose of the article is to:

a) Persuade you to try the GI diet

b) Tell you how to eat healthily

c) Inform you about the GI diet

d) Tell you which foods have a high GI

(1 mark)

2) The article tells you that:

   a)   Low GI foods are bad for you   c)   Chips are a low GI food

   b)   The BNA supports the diet   d)   Diabetes Concern recommends the diet

(1 mark)

3) The picture is helpful because:

   a)   It shows types of low GI foods   c)   It shows that the article is about cooking

   b)   It shows types of high GI foods   d)   It makes the article more persuasive

(1 mark)

4) Which of these statements about the GI diet is false?

   a)   It can help lower blood sugar levels   c)   The GI diet is a balanced diet

   b)   It can help lower the risk of heart disease   d)   Ice-cream is a low GI food

(1 mark)

5) The article suggests that:

   a)   Sugar is banned on the GI diet   c)   The GI diet increases the risk of diabetes

   b)   It's simple to follow the diet   d)   The GI diet is a craze

(1 mark)

6) Identify **three** presentational features that show you that Source B is an article:

   a) ....

      ....

   b) ....

      ....

   c) ....

      ....

(3 marks)

Source C — Australian Wildlife

Read **Source C**, which is a leaflet about crocodiles, then answer the questions that follow. You have 15 minutes to do this exercise.

For multiple-choice questions, circle the letter you have chosen.
For standard answer questions, write your answer in the space provided.
You do not have to write in full sentences. You may use a dictionary.

CROC-WATCH
The NTEA's guide to staying safe

NTEA
Northern Territory
Environmental Agency

The **Northern Territory of Australia** boasts a **unique landscape** and **fascinating wildlife**, but there are a number of **natural dangers** of which you must be **aware** if you are travelling in the area. These include insects, large wild animals and **crocodiles**.

Saltwater crocodiles, or "salties", can be up to 6 metres in length. They live in freshwater estuaries or saltwater environments, such as flood plains, lakes, rivers and coastal waters. "Salties" are aggressive, dangerous and have attacked and killed people on many occasions. However, adult "salties" usually just eat fish, turtles, snakes and livestock.

Freshwater crocodiles grow up to 3 metres in length, and generally inhabit the upper reaches of freshwater creeks and rivers. "Freshies" have a thinner snout than saltwater crocodiles and are dark brown in colour with large body scales. They are usually shy but can become aggressive if disturbed, particularly during the breeding season between August and October.

Use this advice to stay safe

- If you see a crocodile, do not approach it.
- Look out for crocodile warning signs and only swim where it is safe to do so.
- Stand at least 5 metres from the water's edge when fishing.
- Remove rubbish from around your campsite — food can attract crocodiles.
- When camping near water, pitch tents at least 50 metres from the water's edge.

A safer Australia
for everyone   info@NTEA.com.au   •   www.NTEA.au

1) The **main** purpose of the leaflet is to:

a) Inform you about crocodile safety

c) Encourage campers to be tidy

b) Tell you where to spot crocodiles

d) Tell you about different types of crocodile

(1 mark)

2) The leaflet tells you that freshwater crocodiles:

a) Can grow up to 6 metres in length

c) Are always aggressive

b) Breed in September

d) Live in coastal areas

(1 mark)

3) The leaflet suggests that visitors to the Northern Territory:

a) Shouldn't go camping

c) Shouldn't visit in September and October

b) Shouldn't go swimming in freshwater

d) Shouldn't leave food near campsites

(1 mark)

4) Using Source C, list **three** features of the freshwater crocodile's appearance:

a) ....

....

b) ....

....

c) ....

....

(3 marks)

5) Identify **two** presentational features that show you that Source C is a leaflet:

a) ....

....

b) ....

....

(2 marks)

Source D — A Letter of Complaint

Read **Source D** and answer the questions that follow. You have 15 minutes to do this exercise.

For multiple-choice questions, circle the letter you have chosen.
For standard answer questions, write your answer in the space provided.
You do not have to write in full sentences. You may use a dictionary.

You have read this letter of complaint that has been sent to a restaurant you are working at.

LinkedUp Solutions
*Helping businesses work
together since 1994*

LinkedUp Solutions
Greenacre Offices
Steel Street
Portsmouth
PO14 6DS

Sorento's Italian Restaurant
Park View
Portsmouth
PO2 7TD

14th September

Dear Sir / Madam,

I am writing to complain about a bad experience I had at your restaurant recently.
I visited 'Sorento's' on the 8th September for a meal with a business client. I hoped
that the meal would help to build a strong business relationship with the client.

However, our meal was very disappointing. From the moment we arrived, the service we
had was terrible. The waiter, Adam, was rude and he was really slow in bringing us our
food and drinks. The wine glasses were dirty and we had to ask for them to be replaced
twice before clean ones were brought to us. The cutlery also looked as if it had not been
washed properly because it had marks on it.

When the waiter brought the starters, I thought that the situation might improve.
However, my client's starter was brought to the table fifteen minutes after mine arrived.
He had to ask the waiter three times about the delay, which was very embarrassing.
The food itself was quite tasty, although the portions were not very big.

When I have eaten at your restaurant before, the service and meals have always been
excellent. This is why I was so upset about my recent visit.

I hope you will take action to make sure such poor service does not happen again.
I would also like you to respond to this letter with an apology, and include an offer of
a discount for the next time I visit the restaurant.

I look forward to hearing from you.

Yours faithfully,

Jasbinder Singh

Manager, LinkedUp Solutions

1) The **main** purpose of the letter is to:

   a) Ask 'Sorento's' for a refund

   b) Complain about a meal at 'Sorento's'

   c) Build business links with 'Sorento's'

   d) Warn people not to eat at 'Sorento's'

   (1 mark)

2) Which **two** features from the list show that Source D is a letter?

   a) Address and date

   b) Company logo

   c) Full sentences

   d) Formal Language

   e) Using 'Yours faithfully'

   f) Paragraphs

   (2 marks)

3) According to the letter, what was the **main** problem with the starters?

   a) They didn't arrive at the same time

   b) The portions weren't big enough

   c) The knives and forks were dirty

   d) The food was terrible

   (1 mark)

4) According to Jasbinder Singh, what is the service at 'Sorento's' usually like?

   ....

   ....

   (1 mark)

5) Write down **one** thing about the meal on 8th September that Jasbinder Singh enjoyed.

   ....

   ....

   (1 mark)

6) Write down **two** things that Jasbinder Singh wants the restaurant to do.

   a) ....

   ....

   b) ....

   ....

   (2 marks)

Source E — Ant Farms

Read **Source E** and answer the questions that follow. You have 15 minutes to do this exercise.

For multiple-choice questions, circle the letter you have chosen.
For standard answer questions, write your answer in the space provided.
You do not have to write in full sentences. You may use a dictionary.

You have read an advert about ant farms in a pet shop.

ANTICS ANT FARMS — A GREAT GIFT FOR KIDS!

If you want to buy your kids something educational this Christmas, forget about a chemistry set or a stack of textbooks — get them an **ANTICS ant farm!**

You can watch the ants as they build tunnels!

NEW ANT FARMS ON THE MARKET

Imagine an ant farm and you'll probably think of a box of soil — but not any more...

ANTICS ant farms are made up of clear plastic boxes filled with a special jelly for the ants to live in. The box and the jelly are **see-through** so you'll be able to watch your ants making an amazing pattern of tunnels through the jelly. The **whole family** will be fascinated by these brilliant creatures!

FARMS DEVELOPED BY NASA

This particular type of ant farm was developed by NASA who wanted to take a colony of ants into space to study their behaviour. ANTICS ant farms have been **specially designed** to make sure that the ants have **everything they need** to survive inside the farm.

EASY TO CARE FOR

You'll find that your ant farm is simple to look after. It's **clean, safe** and there's **no chance of any ants escaping**. The ants eat the special jelly that they live in, so you don't need to spend extra money on food. The only effort you'll have to put in is finding your ants in the first place. If this seems too much like hard work, you can order specially bred ants.

WHICH ANTS SHOULD I GET?

The best kind of ants for a jelly ant farm are called **Western Harvester** ants.

- Their bodies are large and red so you can easily see them.

- They are strong enough to tunnel easily through the jelly.

- They live for up to three months.

ANT FARMS, £19.99 PLUS P&P, TELEPHONE 07337 987865. BUY TWO ANT FARMS & GET A FREE MAGNIFYING GLASS!

1) The **main** purpose of the text is to:

   a)   Tell you about Western Harvester ants   c)   Persuade you to buy an ant farm

   b)   Give advice about keeping ants as pets   d)   Tell you how to get a free gift

(1 mark)

2) The article informs you that:

   a)   Adults won't be interested in ant farms   c)   Textbooks are better than ant farms

   b)   People of all ages will like ant farms   d)   Ant farms are only popular at Christmas

(1 mark)

3) The article suggests that Western Harvester ants are good for an ant farm because:

   a)   They live for more than three months   c)   They work harder than other ants

   b)   They can build tunnels easily   d)   They can survive in space

(1 mark)

4) Look at the presentation of the advert. Write down **one** way that the advert has been presented and explain why it helps the reader to understand the advert better.

Way the advert is presented ....

It helps the reader to understand the advert because ....

....

(2 marks)

5) Give **three** advantages of ant farms from the advert.

   a)   ....

       ....

   b)   ....

       ....

   c)   ....

       ....

(3 marks)

Source F — Using a Computer Safely

Read **Source F** and answer the questions that follow. You have 15 minutes to do this exercise.

For multiple-choice questions, circle the letter you have chosen.
For standard answer questions, write your answer in the space provided.
You do not have to write in full sentences. You may use a dictionary.

You have read this leaflet aimed at people working with computers.

Tips on Setting Up Your Computer Workstation

Working long hours at a computer can leave you with aches and pains. To avoid developing health problems, people who use a computer regularly should set up their workstation properly.

Your Chair

❏ Adjust the height of the seat so your feet are flat on the floor or you can rest your feet on a footrest.
❏ Adjust the back of the chair to make sure your upper and lower back are supported.
❏ Adjust the armrests so that your shoulders are relaxed.

Your Keyboard

❏ Adjust the position of the keyboard so it is directly in front of your body.
❏ Adjust the keyboard height so that your shoulders are relaxed and your wrists are straight.
❏ Wrist-rests should only be used to rest the palms of your hands when you're not using the keyboard. Avoid resting on the wrist-rest while typing.

Your Mouse

❏ Place the mouse within easy reach of your hand. You shouldn't have to stretch to reach it.
❏ Make sure there is enough space on your desk to move the mouse.

The top of the monitor should be at eye level.

Your Monitor

❏ The top of your monitor should be at about the level of your eyes.
❏ Make sure your screen is at least an arm's length away from your head.
❏ Position your monitor to reduce the amount of glare from the screen. You can do this by keeping it out of direct sunlight.

Tell your manager if you need help setting up your workstation or if you need extra equipment, like a footrest or back support. It only takes a few minutes to set up your workstation properly and even small changes can have a positive effect on your health and comfort at work.

1) The **main** purpose of the leaflet is to:

   a) Tell you how computers work

   b) Warn you not to use computers

   c) Tell you how to position your chair

   d) Give advice about using a computer

   (1 mark)

2) Which of these statements about using a keyboard is false?

   a) It should be in front of you

   b) You should use a wrist-rest when typing

   c) Your wrists should be straight

   d) Your shoulders should be relaxed

   (1 mark)

3) The leaflet suggests that setting up a computer workstation will:

   a) Take a short amount of time

   b) Cause you problems with your manager

   c) Cause you lots of aches and pains

   d) Take a long time

   (1 mark)

4) Who is this leaflet for?

   a) People who have health problems

   b) Managers in the workplace

   c) People who use computers a lot

   d) People who only use laptops

   (1 mark)

5) List **two** parts of your chair that you should adjust when setting up your workstation.

   a) ....

   b) ....

   (2 marks)

6) Identify **two** features that show you that Source F is a leaflet:

   a) ....

   ....

   b) ....

   ....

   (2 marks)

Source G — An Internet Forum

Read **Source G** and answer the questions that follow. You have 15 minutes to do this exercise.

For multiple-choice questions, circle the letter you have chosen.
For standard answer questions, write your answer in the space provided.
You do not have to write in full sentences. You may use a dictionary.

You read a discussion on a webpage about whether shop opening hours should be extended.

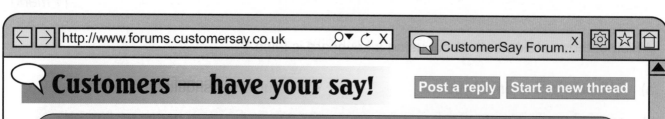

← → | http://www.forums.customersay.co.uk | 🔍▾ ⟳ X | 💬 CustomerSay Forum... X | ⚙ ☆ ⌂

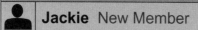

💬 **Customers — have your say!**   [Post a reply] [Start a new thread]

Should shops open later on Sundays?

👤 **Jackie** New Member   Posted: 15th March 17:15

I can't understand why shops don't open for a full day on Sundays — it seems really old-fashioned. The main supermarket in our town closes at 4 pm on a Sunday. This just isn't convenient for many people. I'm a busy Mum who works full time as a nurse. I work long hours during the week and on Saturdays I'm busy taking my son to football practice or walking the dog. I'd prefer to do my shopping on Sunday evening when the kids are at their friends' houses but I can't. I'd definitely support a change in opening hours.

Re: Should shops open later on Sundays?

👤 **Chen** Forum Member   Posted: 16th March 10:26

I understand where you're coming from Jackie, but shopping hours are limited on Sundays for a reason. If you're so busy during the week, Sunday should be the day for spending quality time with your family. It sounds like you could use some time to relax if you're so busy! Can't you plan ahead and do your shopping during the week after work? Think about those people who'd have to work longer hours on Sundays if the law changed — I'm sure they'd prefer to relax at home rather than work until 9 pm on a Sunday evening!

Re: Should shops open later on Sundays?

🐾 **Joel** Forum Member   Posted: 16th March 12:43

Good point Chen. It doesn't seem fair to force people to work on Sunday evenings. Then again, there might be some people who would want that extra money. Also, if longer opening hours mean that shops have to employ more people, that can only be a good thing. The shops that might lose out are smaller supermarkets who can't afford to take on any more staff. They might not be able to open for longer hours on Sunday and could lose out on business.

<u>Contact Us</u> | <u>Register</u> | <u>Forum Rules</u> | <u>Online Safety</u> | <u>Advertisers</u> | <u>Terms and Conditions</u>

1) The **main** purpose of the webpage is for people to:

   a)   Complain about shop opening hours   c)   Persuade others to shop on Sundays

   b)   Share their views about opening hours   d)   Talk about where they go shopping

(1 mark)

2) Joel believes that longer opening hours on Sundays:

   a)   Could benefit some people   c)   Would only benefit small supermarkets

   b)   Would benefit no-one   d)   Would be more convenient for him

(1 mark)

3) Which **two** things does Chen suggest that Jackie should do?

   a)   Work until 9 pm on Sundays   d)   Stop taking her son to football practice

   b)   Take time to relax during the week   e)   Spend time with her family on Sundays

   c)   Go shopping on weekdays instead   f)   Work longer hours during the week

(2 marks)

4) Write down **two** advantages for longer opening hours on
Sunday using the information given on the internet forum.

   a) ....

      ....

   b) ....

      ....

(2 marks)

5) Your friend agrees with Jackie's opinion but you disagree. Using Source G,
give your friend **two** reasons why shop opening hours should not be changed.

   a) ....

      ....

   b) ....

      ....

(2 marks)

Source H — Hoax Calls

Read **Source H** and answer the questions that follow. You have 15 minutes to do this exercise.

For multiple-choice questions, circle the letter you have chosen.
For standard answer questions, write your answer in the space provided.
You do not have to write in full sentences. You may use a dictionary.

You are giving a presentation about hoax callers and read this article in a local newspaper.

The number's up for hoax callers

BY JILL JENKINS
Senior reporter

LOCAL authorities are introducing a new scheme to reduce the numbers of hoax* 999 calls. Nuisance callers, who put lives in danger for the sake of a few laughs, will now be punished by having their mobile phones cut off.

Inspector Tom Bullivant, of Harsham Constabulary, explained, "New technology now allows us to trace the numbers of these hoax callers. Once we identify a number, we have it disconnected. This will inconvenience pranksters and cost them money."

The West Harsham Ambulance Service (WHAS) has received over 400 hoax calls in the last year and an emergency services vehicle was dispatched for almost half of these prank calls. As well

as putting lives in danger, these calls also cost the taxpayer tens of thousands of pounds a year.

Anne Delaney, spokeswoman for the WHAS, said, "Every prank call puts someone's life in danger. Every time an emergency vehicle is sent to deal with a hoax call it wastes time and resources. It means that ambulances and fire engines are not available when someone really needs their help."

The majority of these hoax calls come from children. Inspector Bullivant said, "Parents who give their children mobile phones can help us by making sure their children know that 999 is for emergencies only. We need to

■ TAKING ACTION: West Harsham MP Anthea Bakos

teach children that hoax calls put people's lives at risk."

Local MP Anthea Bakos, has started a campaign to educate young people about hoax calls. "Hospital staff are visiting schools and giving talks to pupils about the consequences of hoax calls," she said. "As well as these talks, we're putting up posters on classroom notice boards and giving students leaflets to make them stop and think about prank calls."

*Hoax — a funny or cruel trick

1) The **main** purpose of the article is to:

a) Tell you about phone tracing technology

b) Inform you about WHAS

c) Encourage you to vote for Anthea Bakos

d) Inform you about hoax calls

(1 mark)

2) The article tells you that:

   a)   All hoax calls are made by children   c)   Most children have a mobile phone

   b)   Most hoax calls are made on mobiles   d)   Hoax calls can be traced

(1 mark)

3) The article suggests:

   a)   An MP is concerned about hoax calls   c)   Hoax callers also target schools

   b)   Hoaxers put taxpayers in debt   d)   The number of hoax callers is rising

(1 mark)

4) The article suggests that:

   a)   Parents are to blame for hoax calls   c)   Hoaxers risk the lives of hospital staff

   b)   Hoaxers think that prank calls are funny   d)   Parents shouldn't give children mobiles

(1 mark)

5) Give **two** reasons why local authorities want to cut down the number of hoax callers:

   a)   ....

       ....

   b)   ....

       ....

(2 marks)

6) Give **two** ways Anthea Bakos is teaching children about hoax calls:

   a)   ....

       ....

   b)   ....

       ....

(2 marks)

Source I — Mifton Film Museum

Read **Source I,** which is a leaflet for Mifton Film Museum, then answer the questions that follow.
You have 15 minutes to do this exercise

For multiple-choice questions, circle the letter you have chosen.
For standard answer questions, write your answer in the space provided.
You do not have to write in full sentences. You may use a dictionary.

ABOUT THE MUSEUM

Based on the site of an old film studio, the Mifton Film Museum has been welcoming visitors for over 25 years. There's plenty to see and do, so come and join us for a great day out for the whole family!

FOR YOUNGER VISITORS

There's plenty for little film-lovers to do. Future movie stars can have their photo taken and turn it into their very own movie poster, or they can try their hand at acting on our film set. There's also plenty of behind-the-scenes activities for kids to get stuck into, with a big costume department for them to raid and an art studio where they can have a go at painting scenery. We offer lots of activities for children, so we're an ideal venue for school trips — please contact us directly to make an enquiry.

FACILITIES

The Director's Cut Café sells a range of food between 10 am - 4 pm every day. If you'd prefer to bring your own lunch, there are picnic tables both inside and outside for you to use.

The museum is fully wheelchair accessible.

Visit our website www.MiftonFilmMuseum.co.uk and get 20% off an online booking.

WHAT'S ON

- Discover the history of cinema with our hands-on exhibit.

- Visit our 'Way Out West' display which features props and costumes from lots of famous westerns.

- Pose with lifelike waxworks of some of the most famous actors and actresses of all time on our very own red carpet.

- Watch a classic movie in our cinema every day at 3 pm.

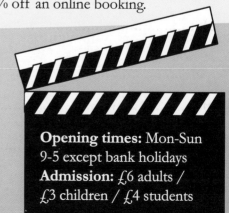

Opening times: Mon-Sun 9-5 except bank holidays
Admission: £6 adults / £3 children / £4 students

(04229) 222 777   ENQUIRIES@MIFTONFILM.CO.UK

1) The **main** purpose of the leaflet is to:

   a) Tell you about the history of cinema

   b) Persuade you to visit the museum

   c) Tell you where the museum is

   d) Inform you about wheelchair facilities

   (1 mark)

2) The leaflet tells you that the museum:

   a) Has been open for less than 25 years

   b) Opens at 10 am

   c) Has its own cinema

   d) Is open on bank holidays

   (1 mark)

3) The 'Facilities' section tells you:

   a) The café is expensive

   b) Food is served between 9 am and 5 pm

   c) There are picnic tables outside

   d) Lots of guests bring their own lunches

   (1 mark)

4) The 'What's On' section tells you:

   a) The 'Way Out West' display is hands-on

   b) They have waxworks of famous directors

   c) You can learn about being an actor

   d) One classic film is shown each day

   (1 mark)

5) According to the leaflet, how can you get a discount on a booking?

   ....

   ....

   (1 mark)

6) List **three** things the leaflet suggests children could do:

   a) ....

   ....

   b) ....

   ....

   c) ....

   ....

   (3 marks)

Source J — Confirmation Letter

Read **Source J** and answer the questions that follow. You have 15 minutes to do this exercise.

For multiple-choice questions, circle the letter you have chosen.
For standard answer questions, write your answer in the space provided.
You do not have to write in full sentences. You may use a dictionary.

You have booked a place on a coach trip to London and have been sent this letter.

Tour • Trek • Travel

Totally Tours,
Tate Road,
Preston,
PR4 8YG
18th March

Dear Traveller,

Thank you for booking a coach trip with Totally Tours. We hope that you have a pleasant holiday and enjoy your time in London. Before you travel, please take some time to read the following information to make sure you are prepared for your trip.

Transport

You and your fellow travellers will be picked up at 10.30 am on Saturday 15th April outside Greenbridge Bus Depot. Please make sure you show your booking confirmation to the coach driver. The journey to London will take approximately 5 hours, including a 30 minute break at a service station.

Arrival in London

We hope to arrive in London by 3.30 pm where you will be taken to The Devonshire Hotel to check in. You will then be shown to your 4-star room where you will have a couple of hours of free time. Your tour guide will meet you in the lobby of the hotel at 5.30 pm to give you a full timetable of the week's activities.

Important information

Please note that the cost of the trip covers the journey, 4 nights stay in a hotel, and all entry fees into museums and galleries. Travellers are expected to cover the cost of food, drinks and souvenirs themselves.

If you wish to cancel your trip, please telephone our hotline as soon as you can.
Note that if you cancel within 24 hours of departure we will be unable to process a refund.

For more information, please visit our website www.TotallyTours.co.uk.

Yours faithfully,

Antonia Muller

Antonia Muller
Managing Director of Totally Tours

1) The **main** purpose of the letter is to:

   a) Persuade you to go on a trip to London

   b) Inform you about your trip to London

   c) Explain where to catch the coach

   d) Tell you about activities to do in London

   (1 mark)

2) The 'Arrival in London' section tells you:

   a) You will have a double bed

   b) You will arrive at 5.30 pm

   c) You will have a free evening

   d) You will stay at The Devonshire Hotel

   (1 mark)

3) The letter tells you that the tour guide:

   a) Is called Antonia Muller

   b) Will need your booking confirmation

   c) Will meet you at Greenbridge Bus Depot

   d) Will give you information about activities

   (1 mark)

4) According to the letter, what date does the tour depart?

   ....

   (1 mark)

5) According to the letter, what should you do if you want to cancel your trip?

   ....

   (1 mark)

6) List **three** things included in the price of the trip:

   a) ....

   ....

   b) ....

   ....

   c) ....

   ....

   (3 marks)

Source K — Internet Shopping Advice

Read **Source K** and then answer the questions that follow. You have 15 minutes to do this exercise.

For multiple-choice questions, circle the letter you have chosen.
For standard answer questions, write your answer in the space provided.
You do not have to write in full sentences. You may use a dictionary.

You find a website giving people advice on internet shopping.

http://www.theonlineadvicecentre.co.uk

the online advice centre .co.uk

- Home
- Shopping
- Banking
- Chat Rooms
- Viruses
- Identity Theft
- Email
- Contact Us

Safe Shopping Online

Internet shopping is big business. More than half of the adults in the UK now shop on the internet, and £1 in every £10 is spent online. This means it is more important than ever to make sure you shop safely online. Ask yourself the following questions every time you visit an internet shopping website.

Is this the best price?

One of the great things about the internet is that you can easily compare the price of an item in a number of places without having to walk all over town. Shop around and make sure the price you're paying is the best out there.

How much will delivery cost?

You might find what you're looking for at a really low price. However, there will usually be a delivery charge to have the item sent. These charges can be anything from a few pence to several pounds, so make sure you check them before you buy anything.

Are my details safe?

To buy something online, you'll usually pay using a credit or debit card. Before you enter your card details, check that the website address starts with https://. There should also be a padlock symbol at the top of the screen, next to the address bar, to show you the website is safe.

Can I return the item?

Before you buy, read the returns policy of the website you're buying from. All shops have to refund the cost of items that are faulty. However, they might not let you return something if you've just changed your mind.

Remember: if you're not sure about a website, don't use it.

1) The **main** purpose of the text is to:

    a)   Tell people about shopping safely online   c)   Tell people how many adults shop online

    b)   Persuade people to use the internet   d)   Tell people how to return items

(1 mark)

2) The text tells you that:

    a)   Shops must refund faulty items   c)   It is hard to compare prices online

    b)   More adults than children shop online   d)   Delivery charges are always similar

(1 mark)

3) Choose **two** features from the list below that show you that the text is a webpage.

    a)   Subheadings

    b)   Coloured text

    c)   Address bar

    d)   Company logo

    e)   Links

    f)   Interesting fonts

(2 marks)

4) Your friend is worried that shopping online is too expensive. What **two** pieces of advice from the article could you give her so that she gets the best price online?

    a) ....

        ....

    b) ....

        ....

(2 marks)

5) Give **two** ways that you can check that your card details will be safe.

    a) ....

        ....

    b) ....

        ....

(2 marks)

Reading Test Practice

Source L — Working in America

Read **Source L** and then answer the questions. You have 15 minutes to do this exercise.

For multiple-choice questions, circle the letter you have chosen.
For standard answer questions, write your answer in the space provided.
You do not have to write in full sentences. You may use a dictionary.

You are thinking about working abroad in America.

Working in the USA

Many people want to travel and experience life in another country, but can't afford to take time off work. Growing numbers of people are choosing to work in another country for a year or so before returning to the UK. The USA is an attractive option for many of these people. Its stunning scenery and lively cities make it a popular destination. The people speak English and the culture is similar to the UK, so most people find it easy to settle there.

Temporary Work Visas

To work in the USA you'll need a temporary work visa. You can apply for one at the US embassy in London. You'll usually have to apply for a job before you arrive in America. The work could be similar to your current job, or it could be totally different. There are loads of options, so think carefully about what you would like to do, and how long you would like to stay in America.

Getting Help

There are travel companies that will organise a job for you. They will charge a fee, but they can also organise your flights and accommodation. All you have to do is let them know when you want to travel, and the types of jobs you are interested in. Some companies even organise trips to tourist attractions so you can see more of the country while you are there. These companies all charge different amounts and offer different services, so shop around to find the one that's best for you.

For more information, visit our website at **www.workingintheusa.co.uk**

1) The **main** purpose of the leaflet is to:

    a)   Persuade people to get a job   c)   Tell people about working in the USA

    b)   Tell people about temporary work visas   d)   Persuade people to travel more

(1 mark)

2) Which of these statements is true?

    a)   You can work in the US without a visa   c)   Travel companies won't organise flights

    b)   Most people find settling in difficult   d)   You can get a visa at the US embassy

(1 mark)

3) What is the **main** point of the 'Getting Help' section?

    a)   Travel companies can organise your trip   c)   Travel companies charge different fees

    b)   It can be hard to get a job in America   d)   People shouldn't pay a company to help

(1 mark)

4) Using the leaflet, give **two** reasons why America is a popular place for British people to work:

    a) ....

       ....

    b) ....

       ....

(2 marks)

5) Your friend wants to work in the USA. Using the leaflet, give **three** things that she should think about before she goes.

    a) ....

       ....

    b) ....

       ....

    c) ....

       ....

(3 marks)

Answers to the Reading Questions

Section One — How Texts Present Ideas

Page 7
Q1 b — A home shopping company
Q2 a — 2002
Q3 You could write any of these:
- London
- Birmingham
- Newport

Q4 a) Informative
b) You could write any of these:
- It gives you information
- It doesn't tell you how to do anything
- It's full of facts

Page 9
Q1 d — From lots of different countries
Q2 c — Over thirty
Q3 Three
Q4 Monday
Q5 a) Persuasive
b) You could write any of these:
- It's trying to persuade people to go to the festival
- It uses persuasive language
- It doesn't use descriptive language

Page 11
Q1 a) Personal
b) You could write any of these:
- He uses the words 'I' and 'we'
- It sounds like it is talking to the reader
- It says what Reginald Sprint thinks

Q2 d — To show that the writer cares
Q3 a) Formal
b) You could write any of these:
- It sounds serious
- It sounds professional
- It isn't chatty
- It doesn't use slang
- It doesn't use shortened words

Q4 a — It sounds more business-like

Page 15
Q1 d — Give ideas for party games to play
Q2 You could write any of these:
- Coloured writing
- Cartoon boat
- Pictures in the title
- Fun fonts

Q3 You could write any 2 of these:
- Subheadings
They break up the text

- Bullet points
Makes the commands clearer
- Title
Says what the text is about
- Different font colours or sizes, bold or underlined text
They break up the text and make it more interesting
- The commands are in a box
This shows they are important
- Short sections
This makes it easier to read
- Cartoon boat
Shows what the game is about

Page 17
Q1 Email
Q2 You could write any of these:
- 'To' box
- 'Subject' box
- A box for the email
- 'Send' button or 'envelope' button

Q3 Website
Q4 You could write any of these:
- Address bar
- Search box
- Links to other pages or 'home' button
- 'Refresh' button
- 'Forward' and 'Back' arrows

Q5 Advert
Q6 You could write any of these:
- Bullet points
- Coloured writing
- Picture
- Interesting font
- Persuasive writing

Q7 Article
Q8 You could write any of these:
- Headline
- Columns
- Subheadings

Section Two — Reading for Detail

Page 19
Q1 You could write any of these:
- Search box
- Links to other pages

Q2 b — To tell the reader about Annette's life
Q3 d — She baked cakes for children's birthdays
Q4 Seventeen
Q5 She admires the courage of firefighters

Page 21
Q1 a — 16 °C
Q2 c — Overcast with sunny intervals
Q3 Western areas

Q4 Southern England & Midlands
Q5 Coastal areas

Page 23
Q1 b — Sunday
Q2 a — To tell people about Joseph's challenge
Q3 c — 6
Q4 c — Go to www.rainhamtimes.com

Page 25
Q1 c — To help people choose a hotel
Q2 a — To persuade people not to stay there
Q3 a) Sandpiper Cottage
b) You could write any 2 of these:
- It's next to a park
- It has a swimming pool
- It has waterslides

Reading Test Practice

You should be aiming to get around six marks and above in these reading exercises to pass.

Source A (Page 26)
Q1 b — Encourage you to buy a car from them
Q2 a — They all live in East London
Q3 c — Prove they have satisfied customers
Q4 c — They are based in East London
Q5 You could write any 2 of these:
- Search box
- Links to other pages
- Menu down the side
- Email mailing list

Q6 You could write any 2 of these:
- Biggest range of used cars
- Best value
- Staff are helpful and polite
- Staff aren't pushy
- Cars are carefully tested
- One year warranty
- 'No fuss guarantee'
- Positive testimonials

Source B (Page 28)
Q1 c — Inform you about the GI diet
Q2 d — Diabetes Concern recommends the diet
Q3 a — It shows types of low GI foods
Q4 c — The GI diet is a balanced diet
Q5 b — It's simple to follow the diet
Q6 You could write any 3 of these:
- Headline
- Text columns
- Subheadings
- Name of editor

Source C (Page 30)

Q1 a — Inform you about crocodile safety

Q2 b — Breed in September

Q3 d — Shouldn't leave food near campsites

Q4 You could write any 3 of these:
- Up to 3 metres in length
- Thinner snout than saltwater crocodiles
- Dark brown colour
- Large body scales

Q5 You could write any 2 of these:
- Text split into boxes
- Use of bullet points
- Use of colour
- Title
- Subheadings
- Different fonts
- Images

Source D (Page 32)

Q1 b — Complain about a meal at 'Sorento's'

Q2 a — Address and date
e — Using 'Yours faithfully'

Q3 a — They didn't arrive at the same time

Q4 Excellent

Q5 The food

Q6 You could write any 2 of these:
- Make sure the poor service doesn't happen again
- Reply with an apology
- Offer a discount

Source E (Page 34)

Q1 c — Persuade you to buy an ant farm

Q2 b — People of all ages will like ant farms

Q3 b — They can build tunnels easily

Q4 You could write any of these:
- Title
It says what the text is about
- Subheadings
They break up the text
- Different fonts colours or sizes
They break up the text
- 'Which ants should I get?' box
It makes the information clear
- Box at the bottom
It makes the details stand out
- Photo
It shows how the ant farm works
- Caption
It explains what the photo shows
- Pictures of ants
It shows what the advert is about

Q5 You could write any 3 of these:
- They're educational
- The whole family will enjoy it
- They're clean
- They're safe
- They have everything the ants need to survive
- The ants can't escape
- They're easy to look after
- You don't need to buy food

Source F (Page 36)

Q1 d — Give advice about using a computer

Q2 b — You should use a wrist-rest when typing

Q3 a — Take a short amount of time

Q4 c — People who use computers a lot

Q5 You could write any 2 of these:
- Height of seat
- Back of chair
- Armrests

Q6 You could write any 2 of these:
- Pictures
- Subheadings
- Bullet points / tick boxes
- Caption
- Heading
- Clear and simple language

Source G (Page 38)

Q1 b — Share their views about opening hours

Q2 a — Could benefit some people

Q3 c — Go shopping on weekdays instead
e — Spend time with her family on Sundays

Q4 You could write any 2 of these:
- It's more convenient
- Some people might want to work extra hours
- Shops might take on more staff

Q5 You could write any 2 of these:
- Sundays are for relaxing
- Sundays are for spending time with your family
- It's not fair on the people who work on Sundays
- Smaller supermarkets might lose business if they can't afford to open later

Source H (Page 40)

Q1 d — Inform you about hoax calls

Q2 d — Hoax calls can be traced

Q3 a — An MP is concerned about hoax calls

Q4 b — Hoaxers think that prank calls are funny

Q5 You could write any 2 of these:
- Puts lives in danger
- Costs thousands of pounds
- Wastes time and resources
- Emergency services aren't available for real emergencies

Q6 You could write any 2 of these:
- Talks from hospital staff
- Displaying posters
- Giving out leaflets

Source I (Page 42)

Q1 b — Persuade you to visit the museum

Q2 c — Has its own cinema

Q3 c — There are picnic tables outside

Q4 d — One classic film is shown each day

Q5 Book tickets online

Q6 You could write any 3 of these:
- Have a photo turned into a movie poster
- Act on the film set
- Raid the costume department
- Paint scenery

Source J (Page 44)

Q1 b — Inform you about your trip to London

Q2 d — You will stay at The Devonshire Hotel

Q3 d — Will give you information about activities

Q4 Saturday 15th April

Q5 Telephone the hotline

Q6 You could write any 3 of these:
- The journey
- The stay in the hotel
- Entry to museums
- Entry to galleries

Source K (Page 46)

Q1 a — Tell people about shopping safely online

Q2 a — Shops must refund faulty items

Q3 c — Address bar
e — Links

Q4 • Shop around
- Check the delivery charge

Q5 • Check for https://
- Check for the padlock symbol

Source L (Page 48)

Q1 c — Tell people about working in the USA

Q2 d — You can get a visa at the US embassy

Q3 a — Travel companies can organise your trip

Q4 You could write any 2 of these:
- Stunning scenery
- Lively cities
- People speak English
- The culture is similar

Q5 You could write any 3 of these:
- What they would like to do
- How long they want to stay
- When they want to travel
- Using a travel company
- Getting a visa

Answers to the Reading Questions

Knowing your Audience and Purpose

Audience and purpose are important

1) The **audience** is the **person** who reads a text.

2) You need to know **who** your audience is so that you know what **style** to write in.

3) The **purpose** is the **reason** a text is written. For example, to **inform** or **describe**.

4) The purpose of a text tells you **what** to write about and **how** to write it.

Find out who you are writing for and why

The question will tell you **who** the text is for (audience) and **why** you are writing it (purpose).

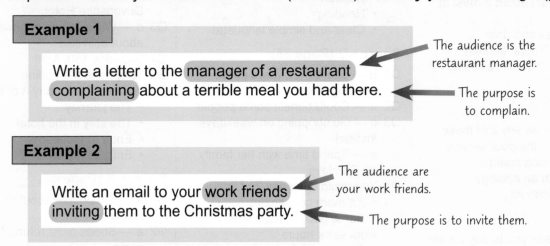

Example 1

Write a letter to the manager of a restaurant complaining about a terrible meal you had there.

The audience is the restaurant manager.

The purpose is to complain.

Example 2

Write an email to your work friends inviting them to the Christmas party.

The audience are your work friends.

The purpose is to invite them.

Use the correct writing style

Make sure the way you write **fits** the audience and the purpose.

See p.10 for more on style.

Example

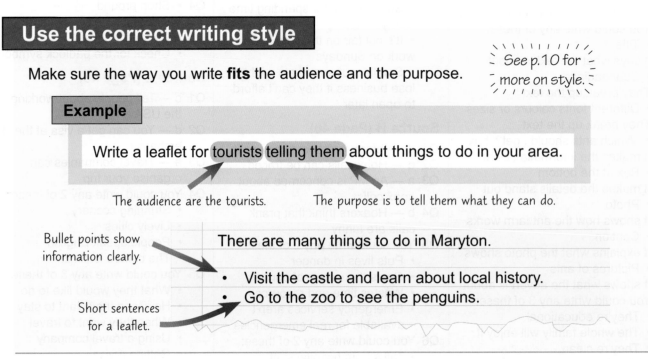

Write a leaflet for tourists telling them about things to do in your area.

The audience are the tourists.

The purpose is to tell them what they can do.

Bullet points show information clearly.

Short sentences for a leaflet.

There are many things to do in Maryton.

- Visit the castle and learn about local history.
- Go to the zoo to see the penguins.

Practice Questions

1) Write down the audience and purpose for each of these writing tasks.

   a) The boiler in your flat has broken. Write an email to your landlord asking him to fix it.

   Audience ....

   Purpose ....

   b) Write an email to your manager asking for time off work to go to the dentist.

   Audience ....

   Purpose ....

   c) Write a letter to the council asking them to fix the potholes on your road.

   Audience ....

   Purpose ....

   d) Write a letter applying for a job in a shop.

   Audience ....

   Purpose ....

   e) Write a newspaper article arguing that speed limits in town centres should be lower.

   Audience ....

   Purpose ....

2) Formal writing is for people you don't know or people in charge.
   Informal writing is for people you know well.

   What type of writing style would you use for these writing tasks? Circle 'Formal' or 'Informal'.

   a) A letter to your best friend describing your holiday   Formal / Informal

   b) An email to your manager about your annual review   Formal / Informal

   c) A letter of complaint to a bus company   Formal / Informal

   d) A thank you letter to your Gran for a birthday present   Formal / Informal

   e) An email to your bank manager about your overdraft   Formal / Informal

Planning your Answer

Make a plan before you start writing

1) Planning your answer will help you put your ideas **in order**.

2) Make sure you **only** write down points that **answer the question**.

3) Making a plan will help you give your answer a **clear** beginning, middle and end.

Write your plan using notes

1) Write your points down and give them an **order**.

2) For instructions, you should put your points in the **order** the reader needs to **do them**.

3) For other writing tasks, you should **organise** your points in order of **importance**.

Example

Write an email to your landlord telling him about the problems in your flat.

Most important point comes first.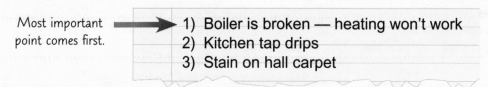

1) Boiler is broken — heating won't work
2) Kitchen tap drips
3) Stain on hall carpet

4) Using a **spider diagram** might help you see how points are **connected**.

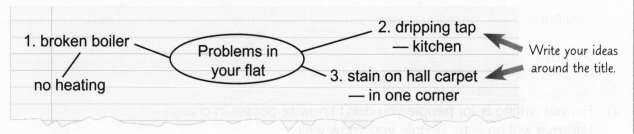

1. broken boiler

no heating

Problems in your flat

2. dripping tap — kitchen

3. stain on hall carpet — in one corner

Write your ideas around the title.

How to plan a letter

1) Work out who the audience is to help decide if the letter should be **formal** or **informal**.

2) This will help you decide which **greeting** and **ending** to use.

3) Your first paragraph should tell the reader the **purpose** of the letter.

See p.64 for more on letters.

4) The main body of the letter **develops** your ideas and gives more **detail**.

5) The last paragraph should tell the reader what **action** you want them to take.

Planning your Answer

How to plan an email

1) Think about **who** is going to read the email. This is your **audience**.

2) This will help you work out if your style should be **formal** or **informal**. 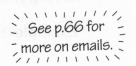 *See p.66 for more on emails.*

3) The **first point** in your plan should be the **purpose** of the email.

4) Write a **paragraph** in the email for **each** point in your plan.

How to plan an article

Work out your **purpose** and **audience**. Think about **where** the article will be printed.

Example

The audience for this article will be a group of people — the charity members.

Write an article for a charity newsletter about an upcoming fund raising activity.

Start with the main facts. What happened, where, when and who?

Audience: newsletter readers   Purpose: to inform

1) Sponsored hike / Mount Snowdon / 6th Aug / four of us
2) 35 km / raising money for hospice
3) Need £500 for new equipment

Then go into detail about the event.

How to plan a report

The purpose of a report is to **give information**. It needs to be **clear** and **accurate**.

Example

Use formal language for reports.

Your co-worker has had an accident at work. Write a report for the Safety Officer telling them what happened.

Injury: broken leg, sprained wrist
Cause: ladder slipped, fell onto floor
Solution: safety ladder, signs, more training

Divide the information clearly into sections.

Planning your Answer

How to plan a leaflet

1) Before you start planning, think about what information the audience **needs**.

> **Example**
>
> Write a leaflet giving people advice on how to improve home security.

2) Start by telling the reader the **purpose** of the leaflet.

3) In your plan, write a **list** of points. Make sure they are **all** relevant.

4) **Number** your points in order from **most** to **least important**.

5) End with a **reminder** about **why** the audience needs to think about the subject.

How to plan a CV

Your CV gives an employer **information about you**. It should be **formal** and **factual**.

Personal Details:	name / address / telephone number / date of birth
Education:	most recent school or college, qualifications and grades
Work history:	jobs (start with most recent) / work experience
Other achievements and hobbies	
References	

Divide your plan into sections. This makes your CV easier to structure.

How to fill in forms

1) Read the **instructions** before you start and make sure you **follow them**.

2) Carefully fill in **every part** of the form. Write '**n/a**' if something doesn't apply to you.

3) If you are asked about your **education** or **jobs**, start with the **most recent** first.

4) For **longer answers**, write a **rough plan** before filling in the form.

Practice Question

1) You are working at a call centre for an internet company. There have been some complaints from customers about the way staff speak to them on the phone.

Write a leaflet giving advice to call centre staff about how to treat customers on the phone.

You should include advice about:

- what staff should do

- what staff should not do

- why it is important to deal with customers politely

Write your plan here. Remember to think about how to divide up the information.

Drafting and Checking

Use your plan to make a first draft

1) Put the ideas in your plan into **full sentences**.

2) Group sentences about the **same thing** into paragraphs.

3) Use the same **order** and **structure** you decided on in your plan.

4) Make sure your writing style is right for your **audience and purpose**.

Keep track of how much time you've spent planning — you might not have time for a draft in the test.

Improve your writing by redrafting it

1) Read over your first draft carefully and **make improvements**.

2) Take out anything you **don't need**.

3) Add in extra details that **improve** your answer and make it **more interesting**.

4) Check that your **spelling, punctuation and grammar** are correct.

Example

Many street lights in your town are broken and have not been fixed.
Write a letter to your local council asking them to improve street lighting.

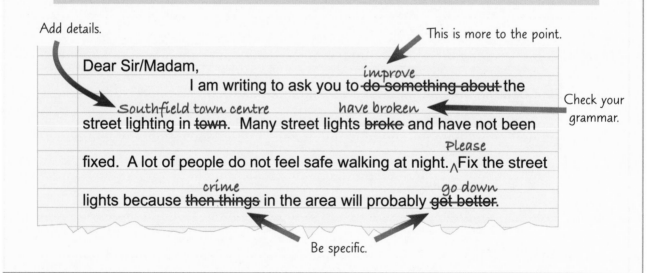

Add details.

This is more to the point.

Dear Sir/Madam,

I am writing to ask you to ~~do something about~~ the *improve*

street lighting in ~~town~~. *Southfield town centre*   Many street lights ~~broke~~ and have not been *have broken*

fixed. A lot of people do not feel safe walking at night. *Please* ∧Fix the street

lights because ~~then things~~ *crime* in the area will probably ~~get better~~. *go down*

Check your grammar.

Be specific.

Check the final draft for mistakes

1) Once you have **corrected** your first draft, write out the **final draft**.

2) Read through it **once more** to check for mistakes.

Practice Question

1) Here is a writing task and an example plan for an answer.

> You are organising a surprise party for your sister's 21st birthday.
> Write an email to her friends inviting them to the party.

<u>Audience</u>: sister's friends (informal) <u>Purpose</u>: invite / inform

<u>Details</u>
- What: 21st birthday party for Sarah, pirate theme
- When: March 25th — early until late
- Where: Brinton village hall — directions / take bus no.34

<u>Anything else</u>
- Costumes / bring themed food and drink
- Other friends welcome
- Keep secret — let me know response by next Friday

Turn this plan into a first draft. Make improvements and add details as you write.

....
....
....
....
....
....
....
....
....
....
....
....
....

Using Paragraphs

Paragraphs make writing easier to read

1) A paragraph is a **group of sentences**.

2) These sentences talk about the **same thing** or **follow on** from each other.

Divide your plan into paragraphs

1) Give each **point** in your plan its own **paragraph**.

2) Start with an **introduction** paragraph. It should **summarise** what your answer is about.

3) Make your last paragraph a **conclusion**. It should **sum up** your main point.

Use paragraphs to show when something changes

1) Start a new paragraph when you talk about a different **topic**, **person**, **place** or **time**.

2) To show a new paragraph start a **new line**.

You can leave a space to show it's a new paragraph.

Different people.

Different place.

> Residents in Newton were woken yesterday morning by loud explosions. ← Start a new paragraph on a new line.
>
> Police arrived to find smoke coming from a local industrial estate. Police dogs were called in to search the area.
>
> In a warehouse in the far corner of the estate, officers found a mountain of fireworks.

Use P.E.E. to develop your points

P.E.E. stands for **Point**, **Example**, **Explanation**. It helps to **structure** your paragraphs.

Make your <u>point</u> first.

Give an <u>example</u> to support your point.

> Riding a bike without a helmet is dangerous. Last week, a cyclist without a helmet was badly injured when they hit a car. Doctors said that their injuries would have been much less serious if they had been wearing a helmet.

<u>Explain</u> how the example backs up your point.

Section One — Writing Structure and Planning

Practice Question

1) Read this piece of writing about Glastonbury music festival.
Rewrite it underneath with new paragraphs in the correct places.

Glastonbury festival is a big music and arts event held in Somerset. Some of the most successful pop artists in history, such as Oasis, U2 and Coldplay, have played there. The festival began in the 1970s and was organised by locals. When a farmer, called Michael Eavis, took over the organisation of the festival, it began to grow in size. Now the festival is held every year, although occasionally there is a break which allows the fields to recover. This means that the fields can still be used for farming. Glastonbury is not just a music festival. It hosts many dance, comedy and theatre acts. There are also sculptures and works of art around the site.

....

....

....

....

....

....

....

....

....

....

....

....

....

Changing your Layout

Layout is a way of making writing interesting

1) Some texts use **layout** to **organise** information.

2) An interesting layout can make the **important points** stand out.

3) It also helps to make a piece of writing **clear** and **easy to read**.

Make sure your layout fits the question

For **articles**, **leaflets** and **reports** think about using different layouts:

> **Example**
>
> Write a leaflet telling people about electric cars. You should talk about the advantages and disadvantages of electric cars.

1) Use **headings** and **subheadings** to give a **clear structure**.

2) The **main heading** tells you what the whole text is about.

3) **Subheadings** break the writing into smaller sections.

4) They tell the reader what **each part** is about.

5) Use **bullet points** or **numbers** for **lists** because they are easy to follow.

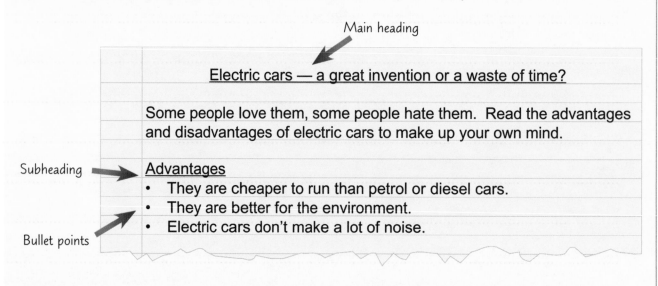

Main heading

Electric cars — a great invention or a waste of time?

Some people love them, some people hate them. Read the advantages and disadvantages of electric cars to make up your own mind.

Subheading → Advantages
• They are cheaper to run than petrol or diesel cars.
• They are better for the environment.
Bullet points → • Electric cars don't make a lot of noise.

Practice Question

1) You have recently started working at a tourist information office.
   They have asked you to write a report about the sports facilities in your town.

   You should write about:

   * what sports facilities there are

   * who uses the facilities

   * what sports facilities you think the town needs

   Remember to use your layout to organise the information in your report.

   ....

   ....

   ....

   ....

   ....

   ....

   ....

   ....

   ....

   ....

   ....

   ....

   ....

   ....

   ....

   ....

Writing Letters

Formal letters are for people you don't know

1) Start with a **formal greeting**. For example, 'Dear Sir/Madam' or 'Dear Mr Jones'.

2) **End** with 'Yours sincerely' if you know their name or 'Yours faithfully' if you don't.

3) Avoid **slang** and **exclamation marks**.

Informal letters are for people you know well

1) Start with the reader's **name**. End with 'Best wishes' or 'See you soon'.

2) You can be more **chatty** but make sure your spelling and grammar are correct.

Follow the rules for writing letters

There are some things that all **formal letters** need.

Example

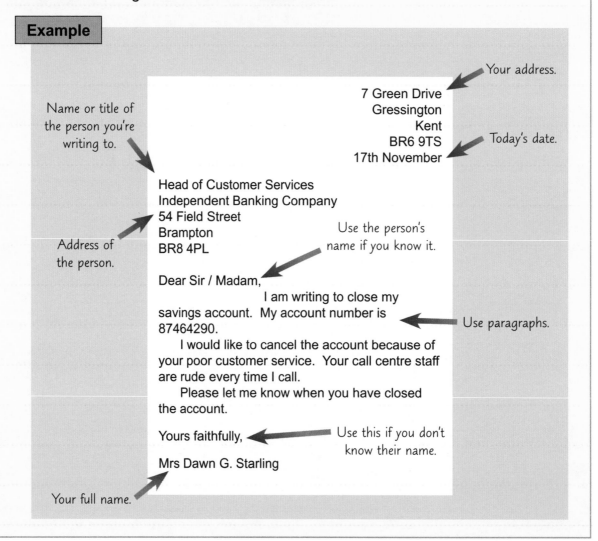

Your address.

7 Green Drive
Gressington
Kent
BR6 9TS
17th November

Today's date.

Name or title of the person you're writing to.

Head of Customer Services
Independent Banking Company
54 Field Street
Brampton
BR8 4PL

Address of the person.

Use the person's name if you know it.

Dear Sir / Madam,

I am writing to close my savings account. My account number is 87464290.

Use paragraphs.

I would like to cancel the account because of your poor customer service. Your call centre staff are rude every time I call.

Please let me know when you have closed the account.

Yours faithfully,

Use this if you don't know their name.

Mrs Dawn G. Starling

Your full name.

Practice Question

1) Write a letter applying for the job described below. Make sure your layout is correct.

> Food Xpress is looking for staff to work on the tills in their new supermarket.
> Staff must be over 16, friendly and hard-working.
> If you would like to apply, please write to the Store Manager, Mr Simon Green.
> The address is Food Xpress, 17 Park Road, Middleton, Surrey, KT8 7MF.

You should include:

- why you would like the job

- why you're a suitable applicant

Writing Emails

Email is electronic mail

1) Email is a way of sending **messages** from one computer to another.

2) You send them to a person or company's **email address**.

> **Example**
>
> brian.mcloud@business.co.uk
>
> The bit before the '@' sign is usually the person's name or title.

Lay out emails correctly

All emails have certain **features**. Make sure you include all the right information.

> **Example**

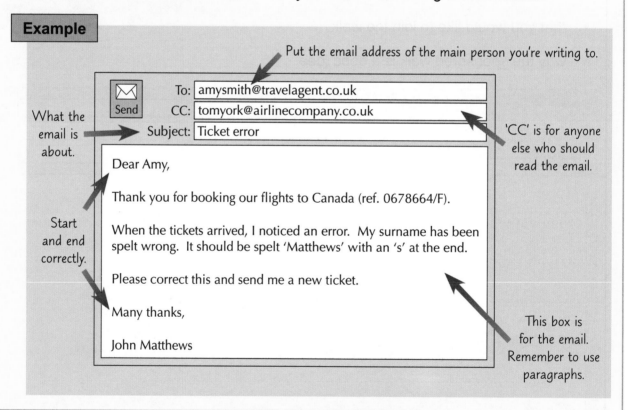

Put the email address of the main person you're writing to.

To: amysmith@travelagent.co.uk

CC: tomyork@airlinecompany.co.uk

Subject: Ticket error

What the email is about.

'CC' is for anyone else who should read the email.

Start and end correctly.

Dear Amy,

Thank you for booking our flights to Canada (ref. 0678664/F).

When the tickets arrived, I noticed an error. My surname has been spelt wrong. It should be spelt 'Matthews' with an 's' at the end.

Please correct this and send me a new ticket.

Many thanks,

John Matthews

This box is for the email. Remember to use paragraphs.

Check that your style is right for the audience

1) When you email a **company** or a **person in charge**, use **formal** language.

2) Emails to **family** and **friends** can be more **informal**.

Practice Question

1) Read this email from a co-worker about a sponsored walk.

From:	karlie.grey@email.co.uk
To:	workers@companyemail.co.uk
Subject:	Sponsored walk

Send

Hello everyone,

I'm doing a sponsored walk on Saturday in the Lake District. The walk is 25 miles long and hilly! I'm walking to raise money for St Mary's Hospital. Can you sponsor me? If you can, let me know how much you would like to give.

Also, does anyone want to join me? Let me know if you do.

Thanks,
Karlie

Write a short reply which says:

• how much money you would like to sponsor Karlie

• that you would like to join the walk

• why the sponsored walk is a good idea

To:	
CC:	
Subject:	

Send

....

....

....

....

....

....

....

....

Using Sentences

Always write in sentences

1) You **don't** need to use full sentences in your **plan**. Use notes instead.

2) You **do** get marks for using **full sentences** in writing exercises.

3) Turn your notes into **full sentences** when you **draft** your answer.

A sentence must make sense on its own

1) Every sentence needs an **action word** and **somebody** to do it.

2) A verb is an action word. It tells you **what happens** in a sentence.

> **Example 1**
>
> This is the verb.
>
>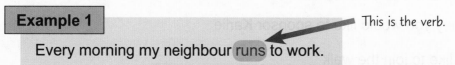
> Every morning my neighbour runs to work.

3) A sentence needs **someone** or **something** to 'do' the verb.

> The machine is doing the action.
>
> **Example 2**
>
>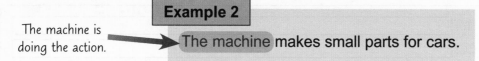
> The machine makes small parts for cars.

4) Extra details tell you **when**, **where** or **how** the action happens.

5) They can also show **who** or **what** the action is being done to.

> **Example 3**
>
> The selling was 'done' to the coin collection.
>
>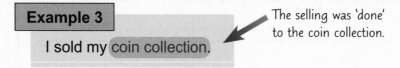
> I sold my coin collection.

Form sentences by putting all the parts together

Put the person or thing **doing** the action and the **verb** together.

> This is the verb.
>
> **Example**
>
> The shopping centre is 'doing' the action.
>
> | The shopping centre | closes | at 11 pm. |
>
> This adds detail.

Practice Questions

1) Underline the verb in each sentence.

   a) We both applied for the same job.

   b) The train arrived seventeen minutes late.

   c) All of our staff wear uniforms.

   d) The secretary types the letters.

   e) Everyone left the building at lunchtime.

   f) I passed my driving test last year.

2) Underline who or what is doing the action in each sentence.

   a) Sometimes dogs howl at the moon.

   b) We waited over an hour for our meal.

   c) Your car makes a strange noise.

   d) On Sundays the leisure centre opens at 10 am.

   e) The manager gave me a pay rise.

   f) I cancelled the order last week.

3) Read these notes from a staff room notice board. Rewrite the notes in full sentences.

   > thefts in staff room last week
   > take care of belongings
   > mobile phones and mp3 players — in your locker
   > if anything missing let manager know

   ....

   ....

   ....

   ....

   ....

   ....

Talking About Things in the Present

A verb is a 'doing' or 'being' word

Use verbs to describe what something **does** or **is**.

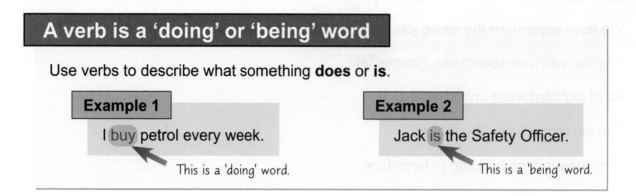

Example 1

I buy petrol every week.

This is a 'doing' word.

Example 2

Jack is the Safety Officer.

This is a 'being' word.

Use the present tense to say what is happening now

Most verbs in the **present tense** follow the same **verb pattern**:

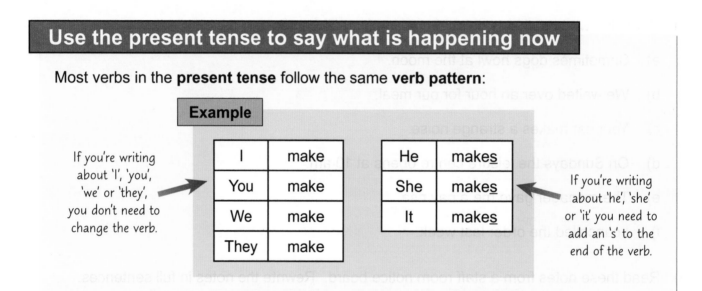

Example

If you're writing about 'I', 'you', 'we' or 'they', you don't need to change the verb.

I	make
You	make
We	make
They	make

He	make**s**
She	make**s**
It	make**s**

If you're writing about 'he', 'she' or 'it' you need to add an 's' to the end of the verb.

How you change the verb depends on who is doing it

Use the **verb pattern** to work out the correct ending.

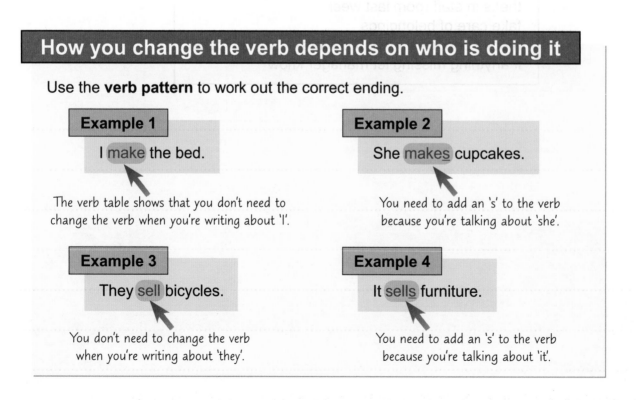

Example 1

I make the bed.

The verb table shows that you don't need to change the verb when you're writing about 'I'.

Example 2

She makes cupcakes.

You need to add an 's' to the verb because you're talking about 'she'.

Example 3

They sell bicycles.

You don't need to change the verb when you're writing about 'they'.

Example 4

It sell**s** furniture.

You need to add an 's' to the verb because you're talking about 'it'.

Talking About Things in the Past

Use the past tense to say what has already happened

1) For most verbs you need to add '**ed**' to the end to make them past tense.

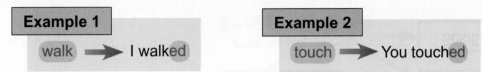

Example 1		Example 2	
walk ➔ I walked		touch ➔ You touched	

2) If the verb already ends in '**e**', just add a '**d**' to the end.

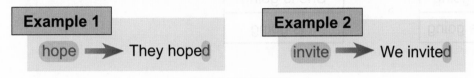

Example 1		Example 2	
hope ➔ They hoped		invite ➔ We invited	

Not all past tense verbs add 'ed'

You need to learn these exceptions.

1) Some verbs follow their own **patterns**.

Examples

Verb	Past Tense		Verb	Past Tense
I do	I did		I am / We are	I was / We were
I have	I had		I go	I went
I see	I saw		I make	I made
I get	I got		I come	I came
I take	I took		I think	I thought

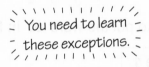

Use 'was' for 'I', 'he', 'she' and 'it'. Use 'were' for 'you', 'we' and 'they'.

2) Some verbs **don't change** at all in the past tense.

Examples

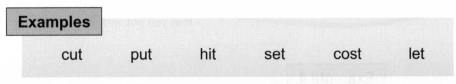

cut   put   hit   set   cost   let

Talking About Things in the Future

To talk about the future you can use 'I am going'...

1) Talk about future actions by using the correct version of '**I am going**'.

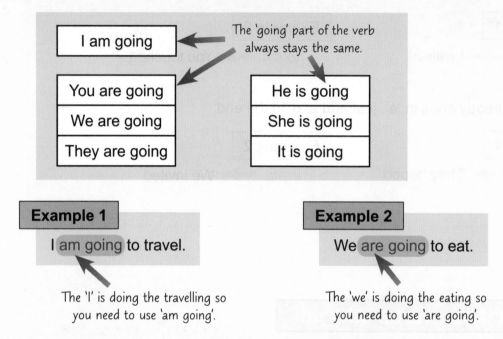

| I am going |
| You are going |
| We are going |
| They are going |

The 'going' part of the verb always stays the same.

| He is going |
| She is going |
| It is going |

Example 1

I am going to travel.

The 'I' is doing the travelling so you need to use 'am going'.

Example 2

We are going to eat.

The 'we' is doing the eating so you need to use 'are going'.

2) You need to put the word '**to**' **in front** of the action being done.

Example 1

He is going to drive.

Example 2

You are going to play golf.

...or you can use 'will'

1) You can also use '**will**' to talk about things in the future.

2) The 'will' part **never changes**. It doesn't matter **who** is doing the action.

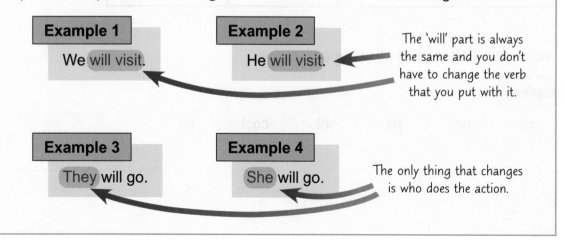

Example 1

We will visit.

Example 2

He will visit.

The 'will' part is always the same and you don't have to change the verb that you put with it.

Example 3

They will go.

Example 4

She will go.

The only thing that changes is who does the action.

Practice Questions

1) Rewrite each sentence in the past tense.

   a) Brian carries a briefcase.

   ....

   b) My friend lives in Bristol.

   ....

   c) I go to the shops.

   ....

   d) The post comes in the morning.

   ....

   e) We do the washing up.

   ....

2) Circle the correct verb to complete each sentence.

   a) Belinda **gives** / **give** the presentation.

   b) Rajesh always **tell** / **tells** terrible jokes.

   c) I **wake** / **wakes** up at 6 am every morning.

   d) Their meeting **was** / **were** very interesting.

3) Rewrite these sentences in the future tense. Use the future tense with 'will'.

   a) I applied for a driving licence.

   ....

   b) The man cycled slowly.

   ....

   c) We were successful.

   ....

   d) You saw the thief.

   ....

Common Mistakes with Verbs

A verb must match the person doing the action

Check **how many people** are doing the action to work out if the **verb** should **change**.

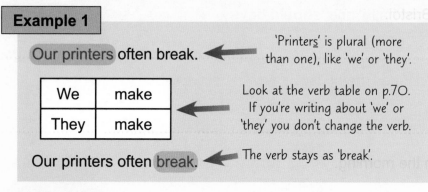

Example 1

Our printers often break.

'Printers' is plural (more than one), like 'we' or 'they'.

| We | make |
| They | make |

Look at the verb table on p.70. If you're writing about 'we' or 'they' you don't change the verb.

Our printers often break.

The verb stays as 'break'.

Example 2

Our printer often break.

'Printer' is singular (one), like 'he', 'she' or 'it'.

| It | makes |

If you're writing about an 'it' you need to add an 's' to the verb.

Our printer often breaks.

The verb becomes 'breaks'.

Use the right 'being' word to go with the person

1) To say 'there **is**' or 'there **are**', use the right **being** word to match the person.

2) Use '**is**' when you're talking about **one person** or **thing**.
   Use '**are**' when you're talking about **more than one** person or thing.

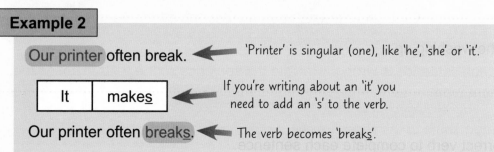

Example 1

There is one security guard.

There is one security guard so use 'is'.

Example 2

There are two security guards.

There are two security guards so use 'are'.

'Been' and 'done' always go with 'have' or 'has'

Always use '**have**' or '**has**' when you write 'been' or 'done'.

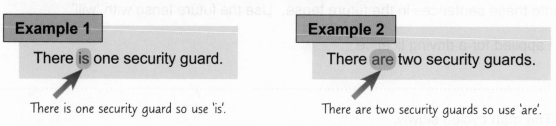

Example

I have done the report you asked for.

You can't miss out the 'have' part. 'I done' doesn't make sense.

Common Mistakes with Verbs

Don't confuse 'could've' and 'could of'

1) Always write '**could have**'. Never write 'could of' because it doesn't mean anything.

2) It's the same for '**might have**' and '**should have**'.

> **Example**
>
> He could have cleaned the house. I should have told him to.
>
> ⬅ It's always 'could have'. You can't say 'could of' or 'could has'.

Practice Questions

1) The verb in each sentence is wrong. Rewrite the sentence so the verb matches the person. Use the present tense.

   a) The women chats to the receptionist.

   ....

   b) Our dogs likes swimming.

   ....

   c) There are just one problem.

   ....

2) Rewrite each sentence so that it makes sense.

   a) We could of tried harder to arrive on time.

   ....

   b) The bank should of told us about the charges.

   ....

   c) I might of lost the key to the filing cabinet.

   ....

Using Joining Words

Joining words develop your writing

Joining words connect parts of sentences **together**.

Example

I enjoy hikes. I like the outdoors. ➡️ I enjoy hikes because I like the outdoors.

Using 'because' makes this piece of writing sound better.

'And', 'because' and 'so' add another point

Use '**and**', '**because**' or '**so**' to add **more detail** to a sentence.

Example 1

I like watching thrillers and comedies.

Example 2

Mel is angry because her train was late. ⬅️ *'because' and 'so' introduce explanations.*

Example 3

Sam is on a diet so he doesn't eat fatty foods.

'But' and 'or' disagree with a point

1) Use '**but**' to **disagree** with something that's just been said.

Example

Marcus usually works the late shift but he is in early today.

2) Use '**or**' to give an **alternative**.

Example

We could go clubbing tonight or we could go bowling.

Practice Questions

1) Choose 'and', 'or', 'so', 'because' or 'but' to complete these sentences.

   a) You can sweeten this with either sugar .... jam.

   b) The shop will be closed both on Monday .... Tuesday.

   c) I can't give you a lift to work .... my car is broken.

   d) My aerobics class is cancelled .... I can come to the cinema.

   e) We could either stay in a hotel tonight .... we could camp.

   f) My dad is only interested in two things, sleeping .... fishing.

   g) I'm scared of spiders .... one crawled on my face as a child.

   h) It's started to rain .... let's walk the dog later.

2) Your cousin has invited you to her wedding ceremony and reception on 28th September. The wedding is at 2 pm and the reception is at 7 pm. You are working until 6.30 pm on that date. Your friend has offered to drive you to the reception after work.

   Write a short reply to your cousin, explaining why you can only attend the reception. Use the joining words 'so', 'because' and 'but'. You don't need to worry about layout.

   ....

   ....

   ....

   ....

   ....

   ....

   ....

   ....

Punctuating Sentences

Sentences start with capital letters...

Every sentence should begin with a **capital letter**.

> **Example**
>
> The price of petrol keeps on rising.

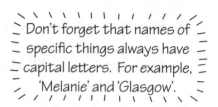

Don't forget that names of specific things always have capital letters. For example, 'Melanie' and 'Glasgow'.

...and end with full stops.

1) Use a **full stop** to show that your sentence has **finished**.

You need a full stop and a capital letter every time you finish one sentence and start another.

> **Example 1**
>
> The car kept rattling. He pulled over.

2) Sometimes you might want to use an **exclamation mark instead** of a full stop.

3) **Only** use an exclamation mark if you're saying something really **amazing**.

> **Example 2**
>
> I realised the exhaust had fallen off!

4) Most sentences aren't amazing, so don't use too many exclamation marks.

5) If you're not sure, use a **full stop instead**.

Questions end with question marks

1) A question should **start** with a **capital letter**...

2) ...but it should end with a **question mark** instead of a full stop.

> **Example**
>
> Are you tired? 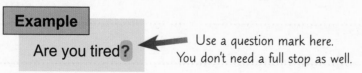   *Use a question mark here. You don't need a full stop as well.*

Practice Questions

1) Use capital letters and full stops to write these sentences correctly.
   You might need to write two sentences instead of one.

   a) She used to go to Cumbria every year

   ....

   b) they only like going on holiday in Britain

   ....

   c) please tell me what your favourite holiday was

   ....

   d) i prefer Wales it never rains there

   ....

   e) we always go to Scotland on holiday it's really warm in the summer

   ....

   ....

   f) My favourite holiday was a trip to Malta it felt like home except it was much hotter

   ....

   ....

2) Use a full stop (.), exclamation mark (!) or question mark (?) to end each sentence correctly.

   a) It's rained for fifteen straight hours, I can't believe it's still raining...

   b) How often does it rain in London...

   c) The rainfall in Cornwall was about average this summer...

   d) It rained so much that I woke up one morning to find the kitchen flooded...

   e) Did you know it was the wettest summer on record...

   f) I think you'll find that it was the second wettest summer...

   g) Have you seen the weather report for next weekend...

Using Commas and Apostrophes

Commas separate things in a list

1) **Commas** can **break up lists** of **three** or **more** things.

2) Put a **comma** after **each thing** in the list.

3) Between the **last two things** you **don't** need a **comma**. Use '**and**' or '**or**' instead.

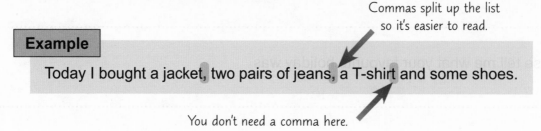

Commas split up the list
so it's easier to read.

Example

Today I bought a jacket, two pairs of jeans, a T-shirt and some shoes.

You don't need a comma here.

Apostrophes can show that letters are missing

1) An **apostrophe** looks like this — **'**

2) Apostrophes show where letters have been **removed** when joining two words together.

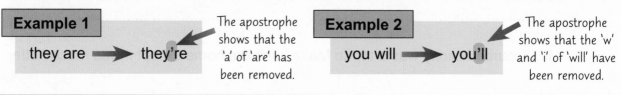

Example 1

they are ➡ they're

The apostrophe shows that the 'a' of 'are' has been removed.

Example 2

you will ➡ you'll

The apostrophe shows that the 'w' and 'i' of 'will' have been removed.

'It's' and 'its' mean different things

1) '**It's**' means 'it is' or 'it has'.

2) The **apostrophe** shows that there are **letters missing**.

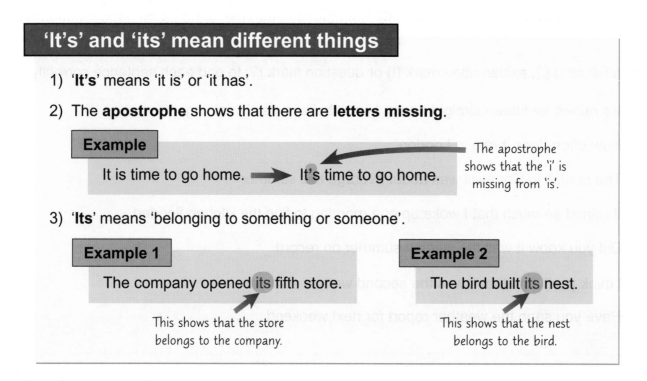

Example

It is time to go home. ➡ It's time to go home.

The apostrophe shows that the 'i' is missing from 'is'.

3) '**Its**' means 'belonging to something or someone'.

Example 1

The company opened its fifth store.

This shows that the store belongs to the company.

Example 2

The bird built its nest.

This shows that the nest belongs to the bird.

Practice Question

1) Rewrite these sentences correctly by putting commas in the correct places.

a) I want to paint my living room either yellow cream or ivory.

....

....

b) The library has books on history art science music and geography.

....

....

c) You'll need a waterproof hiking boots a small bag and a bottle.

....

....

d) The main ingredients are skimmed milk butter and eggs.

....

....

2) Shorten these phrases by putting apostrophes in the correct places.

a) they have ....   e) cannot ....

b) she would ....   f) I am   ....

c) do not   ....   g) he will ....

d) does not ....   h) you are ....

3) Circle the correct word to use in each sentence.

a) The hockey team has cancelled *it's* / *its* Christmas party.

b) Fry the chicken until *it's* / *its* golden on both sides.

c) My phone is broken, *it's* / *its* screen is cracked.

d) Dave says *it's* / *its* really important we get there on time.

Helpful Spelling Tips

The 'i' before 'e' rule

1) 'i' and 'e' often appear **next to each other** in a word.

2) This means it can be **tricky** to **remember** which comes **first**.

3) Use the **'i' before 'e' rule** to help:

'i' before 'e' except after 'c', but only when it rhymes with 'bee'.

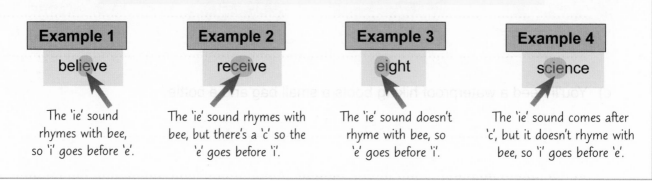

Example 1	Example 2	Example 3	Example 4
believe	receive	eight	science

The 'ie' sound rhymes with bee, so 'i' goes before 'e'.

The 'ie' sound rhymes with bee, but there's a 'c' so the 'e' goes before 'i'.

The 'ie' sound doesn't rhyme with bee, so 'e' goes before 'i'.

The 'ie' sound comes after 'c', but it doesn't rhyme with bee, so 'i' goes before 'e'.

A few words don't follow the rule

Watch out for these **tricky examples**.

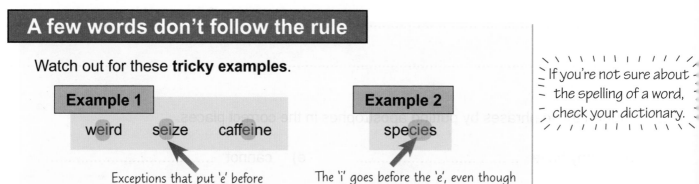

Example 1

weird   seize   caffeine

Exceptions that put 'e' before 'i' that rhyme with bee.

Example 2

species

The 'i' goes before the 'e', even though it comes after 'c' and rhymes with bee.

If you're not sure about the spelling of a word, check your dictionary.

Use funny phrases to help you spell tricky words

Make up **sentences** or **phrases** to remind you how words are spelt.

Example 1

Rhythm Has Your Two Hips Moving ➔ rhythm

The first letter of each word in this phrase helps you spell 'rhythm'.

Example 2

There's **a rat** in separate

Remembering smaller words can help you spell longer words.

Practice Questions

1) Rewrite each word so it is spelt correctly. Some words may already be correct.

    a)   theif   ....   d)   wierd   ....

    b)   neighbour   ....   e)   piece   ....

    c)   cieling   ....   f)   reciept   ....

2) Think of four words that you find tricky to spell. Look up the spelling of each word in a dictionary and write it in the box. Think of a phrase to help you remember how to spell it.

Making Plurals

Plural means 'more than one'

1) To make most words **plural** you add an '**s**' on the **end**.

Example

One car. Two cars.

The 's' means that there is more than one car.

2) If a word **ends** with '**ch**', '**x**', '**s**', '**sh**' or '**z**', put '**es**' on the **end** to make it plural.

Examples

Two churches. Some boxes. Many dresses. Three wishes. The waltzes.

Words ending with 'y' have different rules

1) Some words end with a **vowel** ('a', 'e', 'i', 'o' or 'u') and then a '**y**' (for example b**oy**).

2) To make these words **plural**, put an '**s**' on the end.

Examples

Two days. His keys. Five guys.

All these words end in a vowel and 'y', so they just need an 's'.

3) Some words end with a **consonant** (any letter that isn't a **vowel**) and then a '**y**'.

4) To make them **plural**, change the '**y**' to an '**i**' and then add '**es**' on the **end**.

Example 1

fly → flies

Example 2

city → cities

Words ending with 'f' or 'fe' need a 'v'

1) Words ending in '**f**' can be made **plural** by changing the '**f**' to a '**v**' and adding '**es**'.

Example 1

one shelf → two shelves

Example 2

a thief → three thieves

2) To make words ending with '**fe**' **plural**, change the '**f**' to a '**v**' and add '**s**'.

Example 1

one wife → two wives

Example 2

a knife → three knives

Making Plurals

Some words don't follow a pattern

1) To make some words plural you have to change the **spelling** of the word.

Example 1	Example 2	Example 3
tooth ➡ teeth	woman ➡ women	mouse ➡ mice

2) Some words **don't change at all**.

Examples

fish   deer   sheep

You would always say 'two sheep', never 'two sheeps'.

You need to learn these plurals that don't follow a rule.

Practice Questions

1) Write the plural of each word.

a) comb ....

b) life ....

c) fox ....

d) duty ....

e) watch ....

f) moose ....

2) Rewrite each of these sentences with the correct plurals.

a) The caterers need six loafs for the partys.

....

b) The shop sells penknifes and torchs.

....

c) Please give these ladys their room keies.

....

d) There are a few beachs close to the hoteles.

....

Adding Prefixes and Suffixes

Prefixes and suffixes are used to make new words

1) **Prefixes** are **letters** that are added to the **start** of words.

2) When you add a **prefix** it **changes** the **meaning** of the word.

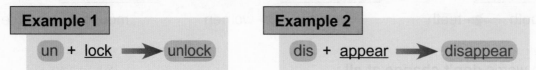

Example 1

un + lock ➔ unlock

Example 2

dis + appear ➔ disappear

3) **Suffixes** are letters that are added to the **end** of words.

4) When you add a **suffix** it also **changes** the **meaning** of the word.

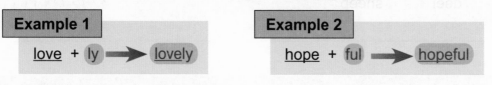

Example 1

love + ly ➔ lovely

Example 2

hope + ful ➔ hopeful

Adding a prefix doesn't change the spelling

If you add a **prefix** to a word, the **spelling** of the **word stays the same**.

The spelling of the prefix and the word don't change.

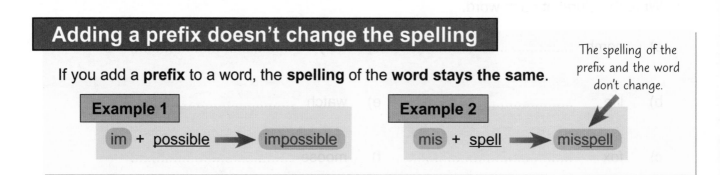

Example 1

im + possible ➔ impossible

Example 2

mis + spell ➔ misspell

Adding a suffix might change the spelling

1) If you add a **suffix** to a word, sometimes the spelling **changes**.

2) If a word ends in an 'e' and the **first letter** of the suffix is a **vowel**, you **drop** the 'e'.

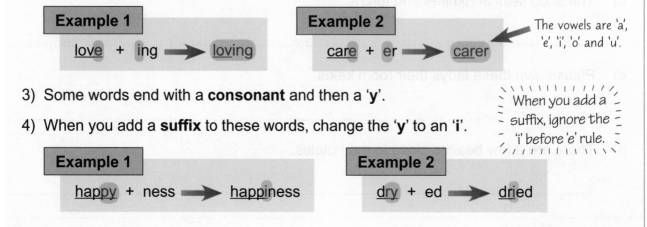

Example 1

love + ing ➔ loving

Example 2

care + er ➔ carer

The vowels are 'a', 'e', 'i', 'o' and 'u'.

3) Some words end with a **consonant** and then a 'y'.

4) When you add a **suffix** to these words, change the 'y' to an 'i'.

When you add a suffix, ignore the 'i' before 'e' rule.

Example 1

happy + ness ➔ happiness

Example 2

dry + ed ➔ dried

Adding Prefixes and Suffixes

The C-V-C rule tells you when to double letters

1) If you are adding a **suffix** that begins with a **vowel**, you can use the **C-V-C rule**.

2) For most words, if the last three letters go **consonant - vowel - consonant (C-V-C)**...

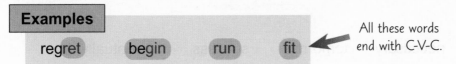

Examples

regret   begin   run   fit

All these words end with C-V-C.

3) ...you **double** the **last letter** when you add the **suffix**.

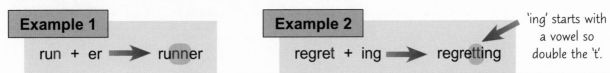

Example 1

run + er ➡ runner

Example 2

regret + ing ➡ regretting

'ing' starts with a vowel so double the 't'.

4) If the **first letter** of the **suffix** is a **consonant** you **don't** double the last letter.

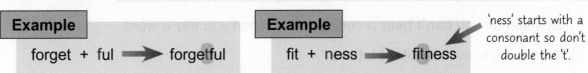

Example

forget + ful ➡ forgetful

Example

fit + ness ➡ fitness

'ness' starts with a consonant so don't double the 't'.

Practice Questions

1) Rewrite each word so it is spelt correctly. Some words may already be correct.

   a) carful ....

   b) happier ....

   c) fatter ....

   d) regreted ....

   e) beting ....

   f) cleverley ....

2) Rewrite each of these sentences and correct the mistakes.

   a) He was takeing his brother to a writting class.

   ....

   b) It's unnlucky that he's missplaced the ticket

   ....

   c) She dissagreed that I'd mispent my youth.

   ....

Common Spelling Mistakes

Words with double letters can be hard to spell

1) It's tricky to spell words with **double letters** because you **can't hear them** when they're said.

2) **Learn** how to spell these **common** words with **double letters**.

> **Examples**
>
> address   necessary   tomorrow   success   eventually
>
> different   possible   professional   immediately   occasionally

Silent letters and unclear sounds can be tricky

1) Sometimes you **can't hear** a certain **letter** when you say a word.

2) These are known as **silent letters**.

> **Examples**
>
> when   which   write   whole   know   could   before   surprise

3) Sometimes the **sound** in a word **isn't clear**.

> **Examples**
>
> because   company   decide   describe   horrible
>
> business   complaint   definitely   experience   interesting

Make sure you learn these tricky spellings.

Make sure you're using the right word

1) **'A lot'** means **'many'**. **'Alot'** is **not** a word.

2) **'Thank you'** is always written as **two words**.

3) **'Maybe'** means **'perhaps'**. **'May be'** means **'might be'**.

If you can swap in 'might be', then you're using the right version of 'may be'.

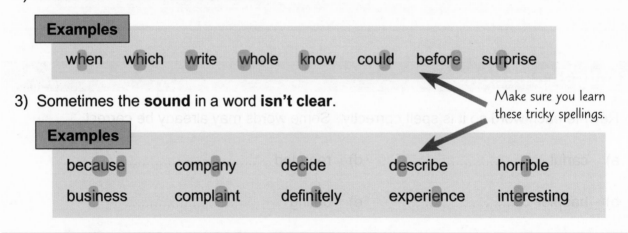

> **Example 1**
>
> Maybe I'll come to the cinema.

> **Example 2**
>
> He may be coming to the cinema.

Practice Questions

1) Each of these sentences has a mistake. Correct the mistake and rewrite the sentence.

   a)   Alot of people think fox hunting is wrong.

   ....

   b)   Thankyou for lending me this book.

   ....

   c)   I prefer to shop on Sunday becos it's less busy.

   ....

   d)   Make sure to include your name and adress.

   ....

   e)   He maybe catching an earlier flight.

   ....

   f)   I suprised my mum with a bunch of flowers.

   ....

   g)   This band plays very intresting music.

   ....

   h)   Wich restaurant are you going to for lunch?

   ....

   i)   Is Maxine definately going on maternity leave?

   ....

   j)   Wen I look after my nephew he's always naughty.

   ....

   k)   Owning a car is unecessary if you live in a city.

   ....

   l)   The salon is open tommorrow from 8 am.

   ....

Commonly Confused Words

'Their', 'they're' and 'there' are all different

1) **'Their'** means 'belonging to them'.

Example 1

Their flat has two bedrooms.

Example 2

He took their warning seriously.

2) **'They're'** means 'they are'.

Example 1

They're living in a two-bed flat.

Example 2

They're giving him a warning.

If you can replace 'they're' with 'they are', and the sentence makes sense, then it's right.

3) **'There'** is used to talk about a **location**...

Example 1

The flat is over there.

Example 2

They are there now.

4) ...or to **introduce a sentence**.

Example 1

There is no reason to give him a warning.

Example 2

There are two choices.

Learn how to use 'to' and 'too'

1) **'To'** can mean 'towards' or it can be part of a **verb**.

Example 1

He's going to Spain.

When 'to' means 'towards', it's followed by a place or an event.

Example 2

Tell him to meet me at 7 pm.

'To' is often followed by a verb.

2) **'Too'** can mean 'too much' or it can mean 'also'.

Example 1

This soup is too hot.

This version of 'too' often has a describing word after it.

Example 2

She's going to the gig too.

When 'too' means 'also', it usually comes at the end of a sentence.

Commonly Confused Words

'Your' and 'you're' mean different things

1) **You're** means 'you are'.

If you can replace 'you're' with 'you are' and the sentence makes sense, then it's the right word.

Example 1

You're working twice this week.

2) **Your** means 'belonging to you'.

Example 2

Keep your uniform in your locker.

The uniform belongs to you.

Don't confuse 'of' and 'off'

1) **Off** can mean 'not on'. **Off** can also mean 'away (from)'.

Example 1

Turn the lights off.

Example 2

I took Monday off work.

2) **Of** is a **linking word**. It **joins parts** of a sentence **together**.

Example

My wardrobe is full of clothes I don't wear.

'Are' and 'our' sound alike

1) **Are** is a **verb** (doing word).

Example 1

We are paid every Friday.

Example 2

Are we going out tonight?

2) **Our** means 'belonging to us'.

Example 2

Our house is near the church.

Example 2

It's our favourite song.

Commonly Confused Words

'Been' and 'being' can sound the same

1) **'Been'** always comes after the words **'have'**, **'has'** or **'had'**.

> **Example**
>
> I have been there before. My mum has been too. Dad had been before us both.

2) **'Being'** always comes after **'am'**, **'are'**, **'were'** or **'was'**.

> **Example 1**
>
> I am being careful.

> **Example 2**
>
> They are being welcomed.

> **Example 3**
>
> We were being friendly.

> **Example 4**
>
> Josh was being protective.

'Bought' and 'brought' mean different things

'Brought' is the past tense of **'bring'**. **'Bought'** is the past tense of **'buy'**.

> **Example**
>
> I brought an umbrella.

This means 'I have an umbrella with me'.

> **Example**
>
> I bought an umbrella.

This means 'I purchased an umbrella'.

Teach and learn are opposites

1) You **teach** information **to** someone else.

2) You **learn** information **from** someone else.

> **Example**
>
> I teach French to my sister.

> **Example**
>
> My sister learns French from me.

Practice Questions

1) Circle the correct word to use in each sentence.

   a) *There* / *Their* were *to* / *too* many people in the park.

   b) If we go to *you're* / *your* house, we can drop off *our* / *are* shopping bags.

   c) He was sacked because he was *been* / *being* rude *to* / *too* the customers.

   d) Lots *of* / *off* people *brought* / *bought* food to the picnic.

   e) They have *been* / *being* painting *your* / *you're* fence for a fortnight.

   f) *Are* / *Our* you going to the cash point? I need to come *to* / *too*.

2) Each of these sentences has a mistake. Correct the mistake and rewrite the sentence.

   a) She was been too harsh with her criticism.

   ....

   b) They're going to have there wedding at the church.

   ....

   c) I bought some shoes but they were to small.

   ....

   d) Switch the computer of when you're finished.

   ....

   e) My friend learns me how to play guitar.

   ....

   f) He bought a box of chocolates into work.

   ....

   g) Harry smashed you're lamp.

   ....

   h) Their buying a new TV to replace the old one.

   ....

Exercise A — Letter of Complaint

You reserved seats on a train, but missed your connection because of delays to the service.
You took a later train, but were made to pay for another ticket.
You have found this information on the train operator's website.

❖ *Advance Purchases* ❖

Be advised that any customer buying tickets in advance must travel
on the train specified. Your ticket will not be valid for other services.

If you have any further queries please write to us at: Railway Services,
Customer Services, 22 Bridgewater Lane, Preston, PR17 6RT

Write a letter to the company complaining about having to pay for the same ticket twice.

You should include:

• What the problem is and why you are unhappy about it

• What you want the company to do about it

Remember to:

• Write accurately and in full sentences
  You will be marked on spelling, punctuation and grammar

• Plan your answer

• Set your letter out correctly

You have 20 minutes to do this exercise. You may use a dictionary.
Write your answer on a piece of lined paper. It should be about 150 words long.   *(10 marks)*

Plan your answer here:

Exercise B — Report on a Local Event

You read this article in a local paper.

Council to Put an End to Fair

The council are considering whether or not to continue funding the local annual fair. The fair, which is a highlight for many locals, has raised over one million pounds for charity since it began twenty-three years ago.

Councillor Green argues that the fair has cost the council almost as much to put on as it has raised. She thinks the money would be better off spent elsewhere, saying that it was "ridiculous to continue funding something so costly just for the sake of tradition."

Write a report for the council, presenting both sides of the argument, to help them decide whether to continue funding the fair.

You should include:

• Why the fair is good for the community

• The arguments against holding the fair

• A suggestion for what the council should do

Remember to:

• Write accurately and in full sentences
  You will be assessed on spelling, punctuation and grammar

• Plan your answer

You have 25 minutes to do this exercise. You may use a dictionary.
Write your answer on a piece of lined paper. It should be about 200 words long. *(15 marks)*

Plan your answer here:

Exercise C — Volunteer Email

You see this advert for volunteers in the local paper.

VOLUNTEERS NEEDED!

Green Warriors are a friendly group of nature volunteers. We do activities such as planting trees and clearing weeds. We meet on Saturday afternoons so if you can spare one afternoon a month please contact Graham Thorp on g.thorp@greenwarriors.org. Tell us a bit about yourself and whether you have any conservation experience. We'd love to hear from you!

Write an email to Graham Thorp telling him you would like to join the Green Warriors.

You should include:

- Some details about yourself

- Why you want to join Green Warriors

- What skills you have that would help with the job

Remember to:

- Write accurately and in full sentences
  You will be assessed on spelling, punctuation and grammar

- Plan your answer

- Set your email out correctly

You have 20 minutes to do this exercise. You may use a dictionary.
Write your answer on a piece of lined paper. It should be about 150 words long.   *(10 marks)*

Plan your answer here:

Exercise D — Hotel Review

You and a friend stayed at the Hotel San Domingo in Spain.
When you come back, you decide to review the hotel on their website.

Write a review of the Hotel San Domingo for their website.

You should include:

* Whether you enjoyed your holiday

* What the hotel was like

* What there was to do in the area

* Anything that you thought the hotel could improve

Remember to:

* Write accurately and in full sentences
  You will be assessed on spelling, punctuation and grammar

* Plan your answer

You have 20 minutes to do this exercise. You may use a dictionary.
Write your answer on a piece of lined paper. It should be about 150 words long.   *(10 marks)*

Plan your answer here:

Exercise E — Application Letter

You see this job advert in your local newspaper and decide to apply.

WAITER / WAITRESS REQUIRED — CHILLIES RESTAURANT

We are looking for a waiter or waitress to greet customers and serve food in our busy Mexican restaurant. Applicants must be friendly and hard working. Previous restaurant work would be a bonus. Chillies is open 7 days a week between 1.30 pm and 9 pm.

If you're interested in applying, please send a letter to the manager:
Juan Torres, Chillies Restaurant, 4 Union Street, Liverpool, L20 4TF.

Please include why you think you'd be suitable for the job, what hours you'd be available to work and any previous experience.

Write a letter to the manager of Chillies restaurant applying for the job.

You should include:

- Why you want to work at Chillies

- Why you would be suitable for the job

- When you are able to work

Remember to:

- Write accurately and in full sentences
  You will be marked on spelling, punctuation and grammar

- Plan your answer

- Set your letter out correctly

You have 30 minutes to do this exercise. You may use a dictionary.
Write your answer on a piece of lined paper. It should be about 300 words long.   *(20 marks)*

Plan your answer here:

Exercise F — Anti-Theft Leaflet

You read this article in the local paper about an increase in thefts in your area.

Theft Increasing in Antley

People in Antley are being warned about a recent rise in crime. According to the police, the number of thefts in public places has risen by 30% in the last two months.

The police are warning local people to keep their belongings safe at all times, and are asking everyone to spread the word to friends and neighbours. They are also asking people to immediately report anything suspicious.

Write a leaflet telling people in Antley how to protect their belongings from thieves when they are in public places.

You should include:

• The items that a thief might want to steal

• The public places where thieves might try to steal things

• How to stop these thefts from happening

Remember to:

• Write accurately and in full sentences
  You will be marked on spelling, punctuation and grammar

• Plan your answer

You have 30 minutes to do this exercise. You may use a dictionary.
Write your answer on a piece of lined paper. It should be about 300 words long. *(25 marks)*

Plan your answer here:

Exercise G — Thank You Letter

You were in charge of organising your work Christmas party this year. It was held at the Bay View Hotel and everyone had a great time. You booked it after seeing their advert.

CHRISTMAS PARTIES at *Bay View Hotel*

Book your Christmas party at the Bay View Hotel and we'll make sure that everyone has a fantastic time! The party package includes:

- A free glass of champagne for everyone
- A buffet which includes vegetarian options
- A disco from 9 pm until midnight
- A private function room with festive decorations

You were really pleased with the food and entertainment offered by the hotel. Write a thank you letter to David Gowan, the Manager of Bay View Hotel, at Cox Street, Fowey, PL23 7PH.

You should include:

- Why you are writing

- The details of your party

- What you liked about the party package

Remember to:

- Write accurately and in full sentences
  You will be marked on spelling, punctuation and grammar

- Plan your answer

- Set your letter out correctly

You have 25 minutes to do this exercise. You may use a dictionary.
Write your answer on a piece of lined paper. It should be about 200 words long.   *(15 marks)*

Plan your answer here:

Exercise H — Appointment Email

You have been given an appointment card by your dentist telling you the date and time of your next appointment. You now realise that you need to change the appointment.

Appointment Card

Purlz Dentist
24 Kenton Road
Manchester
M55 7QR

Appointment date: _Friday 24th July_

Appointment time: _11:30 am_

Name of dentist: _Dr. Raj Amra_

If you need to change this appointment, please email us at mail@purlzmanchester.co.uk

Write an email to your dentist asking to change the date and time of your appointment.

You should include:

- When the appointment should have been and why you need to change it

- A suggestion for when you would like the appointment to be

- What problem you are having with your teeth

Remember to:

- Write accurately and in full sentences
  You will be assessed on spelling, punctuation and grammar

- Plan your answer

- Set your email out correctly

You have 20 minutes to do this exercise. You may use a dictionary.
Write your answer on a piece of lined paper. It should be about 150 words long.   *(10 marks)*

Plan your answer here:

Exercise I — A Newsletter Article

You read this information posted on the noticeboard at your work.

Wanted — articles for company newsletter!

The next edition of the company newsletter, 'Company Matters', is out soon and we need your articles! If you have taken part in an event for charity recently, like the Shepperton Fun Run or the Walking Club's '4 Peaks Challenge', tell the rest of the company about it. Remember to include when and where the event took place and which charity you were raising money for.

Write an article for 'Company Matters' about a recent event you took part in which raised money for charity.

You should include:

• What the event was

• When it took place, where and who did it

• Which charity you were raising money for and why

Remember to:

• Write accurately and in full sentences
  You will be marked on spelling, punctuation and grammar

• Plan your answer

• Set your article out correctly

You have 30 minutes to do this exercise. You may use a dictionary.
Write your answer on a piece of lined paper. It should be about 300 words long.   *(25 marks)*

Plan your answer here:

Exercise J — Music Festival Leaflet

You are part of a group organising a local musical festival. You receive the email below.

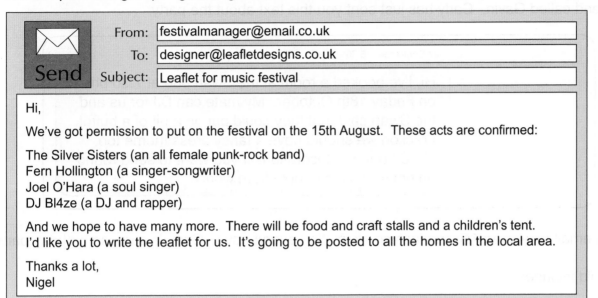

From: festivalmanager@email.co.uk

To: designer@leafletdesigns.co.uk

Subject: Leaflet for music festival

Hi,

We've got permission to put on the festival on the 15th August. These acts are confirmed:

The Silver Sisters (an all female punk-rock band)
Fern Hollington (a singer-songwriter)
Joel O'Hara (a soul singer)
DJ Bl4ze (a DJ and rapper)

And we hope to have many more. There will be food and craft stalls and a children's tent.
I'd like you to write the leaflet for us. It's going to be posted to all the homes in the local area.

Thanks a lot,
Nigel

Write the leaflet to inform local residents about the music festival.

You should include:

*   When the festival is

*   What's on offer at the festival

*   Reasons for people to come along and take part

Remember to:

*   Write accurately and in full sentences
    You will be assessed on spelling, punctuation and grammar

*   Plan your answer

You have 30 minutes to do this exercise. You may use a dictionary.
Write your answer on a piece of lined paper. It should be 300 words long.   *(20 marks)*

Plan your answer here:

Exercise K — Email Invitation

You and your friend Carly have been talking about arranging a surprise birthday party for a work friend called Gavin. Carly has just sent you this text about the party.

27 September 15.36

Hi, I've booked a room at the Swan pub at 7.30 pm on Friday 18th October. My mate can DJ for us and the Swan said that they could put on a bit of a buffet. I reckon we should have a fancy dress theme too. I'll sort out the decorations if you want to send round an email inviting people from work?

Write an email to workers@workplace.co.uk inviting everybody to Gavin's surprise birthday party.

You should include:

• The details of the party

• Reasons for your work friends to come along

• Say what you're going to wear and suggest what other people could wear

Remember to:

• Write accurately and in full sentences
  You will be marked on spelling, punctuation and grammar

• Plan your answer

• Set your email out correctly

You have 20 minutes to do this exercise. You may use a dictionary.
Write your answer on a piece of lined paper. It should be about 150 words long. *(10 marks)*

Plan your answer here:

Exercise L — Letter to the Council

You read this leaflet which was delivered to your house.

Did you know?

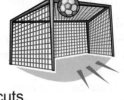

- Council taxes have gone up by **15%** in the last ten years, but community projects have less funding than ever before.

- Public sports fields and parks are being **closed** due to recent budget cuts.

- Recent surveys suggest that areas with a large number of parks, football pitches and basketball courts have a **lower level of crime**.

If, like us, you think that our councillor should fund more community projects, write to Councillor James Bird, 45 Red Lane, Southampton, SO17 8YS.

Write a letter to the councillor persuading him to support more community projects.

You should include:

- Why you think the council should fund more community projects

- Why you think community projects are important

Remember to:

- Write accurately and in full sentences
  You will be marked on spelling, punctuation and grammar

- Plan your answer

- Set your letter out correctly

You have 25 minutes to do this exercise. You may use a dictionary.
Write your answer on a piece of lined paper. It should be about 200 words long. *(15 marks)*

Plan your answer here:

Answers to the Writing Questions

Section One — Writing Structure and Planning

Page 53
Q1 a) Audience: your landlord
Purpose: to ask him to fix the boiler
b) Audience: your manager
Purpose: to ask for time off
c) Audience: the council
Purpose: to ask them to fix potholes
d) Audience: shop owner or manager
Purpose: to apply for a job
e) Audience: newspaper readers
Purpose: to argue for lower speed limits

Q2 a) Informal
b) Formal
c) Formal
d) Informal
e) Formal

Page 57
Q1
• Start with the purpose of the leaflet. It's about improving customer service.
• Write your points in a list.
• Put the most important point first and the least important point last.
• Make sure all the points are about talking to customers on the phone.
• Divide the points into sections. You could use the bullet points as a rough guide.
• End with a reminder of why it's important to be polite to customers.

Page 59
Q1
• Make sure you include all the information from the plan.
• Write in full sentences.
• Your writing style should be informal because your audience is your sister's friends.
• Start with the important details, then write about everything else.
• Add anything else that you think your sister's friends need to know.

Page 61
Q1   Glastonbury festival is a big music and arts event held in Somerset. Some of the most successful pop artists in history, such as Oasis, U2 and Coldplay, have played there.

The festival began in the 1970s and was organised by locals. When a farmer, called Michael Eavis, took over the organisation of the festival, it began to grow in size.

Now the festival is held every year, although occasionally there is a break which allows the fields to recover. This means that the fields can still be used for farming.

Glastonbury is not just a music festival. It hosts many dance, comedy and theatre acts. There are also sculptures and works of art around the site.

Page 63
Q1 Make sure your report has used some of these layout features:
• A main heading to show what the report is about.
• Subheadings to divide the information into sections.
You could use the bullet points provided as a rough guide.
• You could use bullet points or numbers for lists.

Section Two — Choosing the Right Language and Format

Page 65
Q1
• Include your full address on the right-hand side.
• Write the supermarket's full address on the left-hand side.
• Add today's date under your address.
• Use 'Dear Mr Green' to start the letter. Do not use 'Dear Sir / Madam'.
• Use a formal writing style.
• Write in paragraphs. You could have one paragraph for why you want to work at the supermarket, and one paragraph explaining why you're a suitable applicant.
• End with what you want him to do. For example, that you're looking forward to his reply.

• Sign-off with 'Yours sincerely', because you know who you're writing to, and your full name.

Page 67
Q1
• Fill in the 'To' box with karlie.grey@email.co.uk.
• Make sure you fill in the subject box with something suitable. For example, 'Sponsored walk' or 'Great idea'.
• Start with 'Dear Karlie'.
• Write in paragraphs. You could use the bullet points as a rough guide for what each paragraph should be about.
• Use an informal writing style because you know her personally.
• End with something like 'See you soon' or 'Best wishes' and your name.

Section Three — Using Grammar

Page 69
Q1 a) applied
b) arrived
c) wear
d) types
e) left
f) passed

Q2 a) dogs
b) we
c) your car
d) the leisure centre
e) the manager
f) I

Q3 Answers may vary. For example: There were some thefts from the staff room last week. Make sure you take care of your belongings. Leave valuables, like mobile phones and mp3 players, in your locker. If anything goes missing, please let your manager know.

Page 73
Q1 a) Brian carried a briefcase.
b) My friend lived in Bristol.
c) I went to the shops.
d) The post came in the morning.
e) We did the washing up.

Q2 a) gives
b) tells
c) wake
d) was

Q3 a) I will apply for a driving licence.
b) The man will cycle slowly.
c) We will be successful.
d) You will see the thief.

Page 75
Q1 a) The women chat to the receptionist.
b) Our dogs like swimming.
c) There is just one problem.

Q2 a) We could have tried harder to arrive on time.
b) The bank should have told us about the charges.
c) I might have lost the key to the filing cabinet.

Page 77
Q1 a) or
b) and
c) because
d) so
e) or
f) and
g) because
h) so

Q2 Answers may vary, for example:
Dear Fran, I would love to come to your wedding but I can only come to the reception. I can't come to the ceremony because I am working until 6.30 pm. A friend has offered to drive me to the reception after work so I should be there on time.

Section Four — Using Correct Punctuation
Page 79
Q1 a) She used to go to Cumbria every year.
b) They only like going on holiday in Britain.
c) Please tell me what your favourite holiday was.
d) I prefer Wales. It never rains there. ('I' is always a capital, no matter where it comes in a sentence.)
e) We always go to Scotland on holiday. It's really warm in the summer.
f) My favourite holiday was a trip to Malta. It felt like home except it was much hotter.

Q2 a) !
b) ?
c) .
d) !
e) ?
f) .
g) ?

Page 81
Q1 a) I want to paint my living room either yellow, cream or ivory.
b) The library has books on history, art, science, music and geography.
c) You'll need a waterproof, hiking boots, a small bag and a bottle.
d) The main ingredients are skimmed milk, butter and eggs.

Q2 a) they've
b) she'd
c) don't
d) doesn't
e) can't
f) I'm
g) he'll
h) you're

Q3 a) its
b) it's
c) its
d) it's

Section Five — Using Correct Spelling
Page 83
Q1 a) thief
b) neighbour (word is spelt correctly)
c) ceiling
d) weird
e) piece (word is spelt correctly)
f) receipt

Q2 Answers may vary. For example:
Because = Big Elephants Can Always Understand Small Elephants.

Page 85
Q1 a) combs
b) lives
c) foxes
d) duties
e) watches
f) moose (plural is the same)

Q2 a) The caterers need six loaves for the parties.
b) The shop sells penknives and torches.

c) Please give the ladies their room keys.
d) There are a few beaches close to the hotels.

Page 87
Q1 a) careful
b) happier (word is spelt correctly)
c) fatter (word is spelt correctly)
d) regretted
e) betting
f) cleverly

Q2 a) He was taking his brother to a writing class.
b) It's unlucky that he's misplaced the ticket
c) She disagreed that I'd misspent my youth.

Page 89
Q1 a) A lot of people think fox hunting is wrong.
b) Thank you for lending me this book.
c) I prefer to shop on Sunday because it's less busy.
d) Make sure to include your name and address.
e) He may be catching an earlier flight.
f) I surprised my mum with a bunch of flowers.
g) This band plays very interesting music.
h) Which restaurant are you going to for lunch?
i) Is Maxine definitely going on maternity leave?
j) When I look after my nephew he's always naughty.
k) Owning a car is unnecessary if you live in a city.
l) The salon is open tomorrow from 8 am.

Page 93
Q1 a) There   too
b) your   our
c) being   to
d) of   brought
e) been   your
f) Are   too

Q2 a) She was being too harsh with her criticism.
b) They're going to have their wedding at the church.
c) I bought some shoes but they were too small.
d) Switch the computer off when you're finished.

Answers to the Writing Questions

e) My friend <u>teaches</u> me how to play guitar.

f) He <u>brought</u> a box of chocolates into work.

g) Harry smashed <u>your</u> lamp.

h) <u>They're</u> buying a new TV to replace the old one.

Writing Test Practice

These writing exercises are worth different numbers of marks and take different lengths of time to complete. This is because each exam board marks their tests differently. Ask your teacher which exam board you are sitting so you know what to expect in the real test.

Exercise A (Page 94)

You should set your letter out correctly:

• Write your name and address at the top right-hand side of the page.

• Write the date underneath your address.

• Write the full address of 'Railway Services' on the left-hand side of the page:
Railway Services,
Customer Services,
22 Bridgewater Lane,
Preston,
PR17 6RT

• Start with 'Dear Sir / Madam' because you don't know who you're writing to.

• End the letter with 'Yours faithfully' because you don't know the person's name.

• Use paragraphs and full sentences. You should start a new paragraph for each point.

(You get 1 mark for using the correct format.)

Your writing style should:

• Be formal because you don't know the person you're writing to.

• Have a suitable greeting and sign-off for a formal letter.

(You get 1 mark for using a suitable tone and style for your audience.)

You should include this information:

• What the problem is. You missed your connecting train during a recent journey because the first train was late, and you had to buy a new ticket.

• Why you are unhappy about it. You had already bought a ticket for the train and it wasn't your fault that you missed the connection.

• What you want the company to do about it. For example, you would like a refund for the extra ticket you had to buy, some vouchers, an apology or you want them to improve their customer service.

Use a clear structure:

• Start with the purpose of the letter. You're complaining about poor customer service.

• Go on to say what the problem is and why you're unhappy.

• End with what you want them to do. For example, offer a refund.

(You can get up to 4 marks for including suitable content in a sensible order.)

You should use correct spelling, punctuation and grammar.

(You can get up to 4 marks for using correct spelling, punctuation and grammar.)

You should be aiming to get around seven marks and above to pass.

Exercise B (Page 95)

You should set your report out suitably:

• Write a heading to show what the report is about. For example, 'Pros and Cons of the Fair'.

• You could use subheadings to separate the two sides of the argument.

• Group similar points together. You could use bullet points or a numbered list to show information more clearly.

• Use paragraphs and full sentences. You should start a new paragraph for each point.

(You can get up to 2 marks for using a suitable format.)

Your writing style should:

• Be formal because it is a report for the council and it sounds more professional.

• Be informative, so make sure you include all of the facts.

• Be clear because you want the council to understand the arguments properly.

You could be persuasive if you felt strongly one way or the other.

(You can get up to 2 marks for using a suitable tone and style for your audience.)

You should include this information:

• Why the fair is good for the community. For example, local people enjoy it, the fair has raised more than a million pounds for charity or that it is part of local tradition.

• Arguments against funding the fair. For example, it costs the council lots of money to fund it, the money spent on the fair would be better spent on something else, like libraries.

• A suggestion of what the council should do. For example, whether you think the council should or shouldn't fund the fair. Explain why you think this is the best idea.

• You could suggest a third alternative. For example, funding it through donations.

Use a clear structure:

• Start by explaining what the report is about. It's to help decide whether or not the council should continue funding the fair.

• Go on to explain the arguments for and against funding the fair. Group all the arguments for funding the fair together. Do the same for all the arguments against funding the fair.

• End by saying what you think the council should do and why.

(You can get up to 5 marks for including suitable content in a sensible order.)

You should use correct spelling, punctuation and grammar.

(You can get up to 6 marks for using correct spelling, punctuation and grammar.)

You should be aiming to get around ten marks and above to pass.

Exercise C (Page 96)

You should set your email out correctly:

• Write 'To' followed by g.thorp@greenwarriors.org to show who the email is for.

Answers to the Writing Questions

- Underneath, write 'From' and then your email address.
- Write 'Subject' followed by a suitable subject. For example, 'Green Warriors' or 'Volunteers'.
- Start your email with 'Dear Mr Thorp'.
- Sign-off your email with something suitable, for example 'Many thanks' and your name.
- Use paragraphs and full sentences. You should start a new paragraph for each point.

(You get 1 mark for using a suitable format.)

Your writing style should:
- Be fairly formal because you don't know the person you're writing to personally.
- Have a suitable greeting and sign-off.
- Friendly because you want to make a good impression.

(You get 1 mark for using a suitable tone and style for your audience.)

You should include this information:
- Some details about yourself. For example, your name, age, job or where you live.
- Why you want to join Green Warriors. For example, because you are interested in the environment, you like gardening, you enjoy working outdoors or you want to meet new people.
- What skills you have that would help. For example, you are hardworking, have gardening experience or know about nature.

Use a clear structure:
- Start by explaining the purpose of your email. You're interested in joining Green Warriors.
- Go on to give some details about yourself, followed by some reasons why you want to join, and the skills you have.
- End with what you want him to do. For example, that you're looking forward to his reply.

(You can get up to 4 marks for including suitable content in a sensible order.)

You should use correct spelling, punctuation and grammar.

(You can get up to 4 marks for using correct spelling, punctuation and grammar.)

You should be aiming to get around seven marks and above to pass.

Exercise D (Page 97)

You should set out your review suitably:
- Write a heading to show what the review is about. For example, 'Awful Food' or 'Brilliant Rooms'.
- End with your name to show who wrote the review. You could also include where you are from.
- Use paragraphs and full sentences. You should start a new paragraph for each point.

(You get 1 mark for using a suitable format.)

Your writing style should:
- Be descriptive because you want to tell the reader what the hotel was like in detail.
- You could be persuasive if you felt strongly one way or the other.
- Be the same for all of your review. For example, if you start writing in an informal style, don't write some parts in a formal style.

(You get 1 mark for using a suitable tone and style for your audience.)

You should include this information:
- Whether you enjoyed your holiday. You could talk about what you did while you were there, the food and drink or the entertainment.
- What the hotel was like. You could talk about the hotel bar, the outside swimming pool, the gym and the staff.
- What there was to do in the area. You could mention beaches, the local town and any other attractions like a water park or a zoo.
- What the hotel could improve on. You could talk about the cleanliness of the hotel, the day trips on offer or the size and quality of the rooms.

Use a clear structure:
- Start by saying which parts of the hotel you liked or didn't like.
- Go on to talk about what the hotel could improve on.
- End by giving your overall opinion of the hotel.

(You can get up to 4 marks for including suitable content in a sensible order.)

You should use correct spelling, punctuation and grammar.

(You can get up to 4 marks for using correct spelling, punctuation and grammar.)

You should be aiming to get 7 or more marks to achieve a pass.

Exercise E (Page 98)

You should set your letter out correctly:
- Write your name and address at the top right-hand side of the page.
- Write the date underneath your address.
- Write the full address of 'Chillies Restaurant' on the left-hand side of the page:
Mr Torres
Chillies Restaurant,
4 Union Street,
Liverpool,
L20 4TF
- Start with 'Dear Mr Torres' because you know his name from the advert. Don't write 'Dear Juan' as it's too personal. Don't write 'Dear Sir/Madam'.
- End the letter with 'Yours sincerely', because you know the person's name.
- Use paragraphs and full sentences. You should start a new paragraph for each point.

(You can get up to 2 marks for using the correct format.)

Your writing style should:
- Be formal because you don't know the person you're writing to personally.
- Have a suitable greeting and sign-off for a formal letter.
- Be polite as you want to make a good impression.

(You can get up to 3 marks for using a suitable tone and style for your audience.)

You should include this information:
- Why you want to work for Chillies Restaurant. For example, you enjoy working in a busy environment or you like meeting customers.
- Why you would be suitable for the job. For example, you've had previous experience of working in restaurants or you have worked in customer services before.

Answers to the Writing Questions

110

• What hours you'd be available to work. For example, you might only be able to work weekends.
• You could give examples of why you are friendly or hardworking. For example, you had a previous job which had long hours.

Use a clear structure:
• Start with the purpose of the letter. You're applying for the job.
• Go on to say why you want to work there, when you can work, and what skills you have.
• End with what you want them to do. For example, contact you with a response.
(You can get up to 7 marks for including suitable content in a sensible order.)

You should use correct spelling, punctuation and grammar.
(You can get up to 8 marks for using correct spelling, punctuation and grammar.)

You should be aiming to get around fourteen marks and above to pass.

Exercise F (Page 99)
You should set out your leaflet suitably:
• Use a heading to show what the leaflet is about. For example, 'Watch Out For Thieves'.
• You could split the leaflet into sections using subheadings.
• You could use bullet points or numbered lists to break up the text and make the details clear.
(You can get up to 2 marks for using a suitable format.)

Your writing style should:
• Be informative because you want to provide lots of information.
• Be instructive because you want to give lots of advice.
• Use short sentences to make your leaflet easy to understand.
• Be the same for all of your leaflet. For example, if you start writing in an informal style, don't write some parts in a formal style.
(You can get up to 3 marks for using a suitable tone and style for your audience.)

You should include this information:
• The items that a thief might want to steal. For example, mobile phones, money, credit cards or unattended bags.
• The public places where thieves might try to steal things. For example, a cafe, a train station, an airport or a shop.
• How to stop these thefts from happening. For example, don't put things in your back pockets, keep your luggage with you at all times, keep your handbag zipped shut and don't leave your bag on the back of your chair.

Use a clear structure:
• You should group similar information together and put the most important points first.
• Start by writing the purpose of the leaflet, which is to give advice about protecting your belongings.
• Go on to give details about what to look out for, when to be careful and how to protect yourself.
• End with a reminder that people should be aware and stay safe.
(You can get up to 9 marks for including suitable content in a sensible order.)

You should use correct spelling, punctuation and grammar.
(You can get up to 11 marks for using correct spelling, punctuation and grammar.)

You should be aiming to get around seventeen marks and above to pass.

Exercise G (Page 100)
You should set your letter out correctly:
• Write your name and address at the top right-hand side of the page.
• Write the date underneath your address.
• Write the full address of 'Bay View Hotel' on the left-hand side of the page:
Mr Gowan
Bay View Hotel,
Cox Street,
Fowey,
PL23 7PH
• Start with 'Dear Mr Gowan' because you know his name. Don't write 'Dear David' as it's too personal. Don't write 'Dear Sir/Madam'.

• End the letter with 'Yours sincerely' because you know who you're writing to.
• Use paragraphs and full sentences. You should start a new paragraph for each point.
(You can get up to 2 marks for using the correct format.)

Your writing style should:
• Be formal because you don't know the person you're writing to personally.
• Have a suitable greeting and sign-off for a formal letter.
• Be friendly because you're writing to say thank you.
(You can get up to 2 marks for using a suitable tone and style for your audience.)

You should include this information:
• Why you are writing. You want to thank the hotel manager for the food and entertainment at your Christmas party.
• The details of your party. Say when your party was and who your company is.
• What you liked about the party package. For example, you could mention the free glass of champagne, the buffet, the disco DJ, the festive decorations or the staff.

Use a clear structure:
• Start with the purpose of the letter. You want to say thank you.
• Go on to give the details of the party.
• Explain why you enjoyed the party at the hotel.
• End by thanking the hotel manager again.
(You can get up to 5 marks for including suitable content in a sensible order.)

You should use correct spelling, punctuation and grammar.
(You can get up to 6 marks for using correct spelling, punctuation and grammar.)

You should be aiming to get around ten marks and above to pass.

Answers to the Writing Questions

Exercise H (Page 101)

You should set out your email correctly:
- Write 'To' followed by mail@ purlzmanchester.co.uk to show who the email is for. Don't write the street address.
- Underneath, write 'From' and then your email address.
- Write 'Subject' followed by a suitable subject. For example, 'Appointment'.
- Start your email with 'Dear Dr Amra'. Don't write 'Dear Raj' as it's too personal. Don't write 'Dear Sir/Madam'.
- Sign-off your email with something suitable. For example, 'Yours faithfully' and your name.
- Use paragraphs and full sentences. You should start a new paragraph for each point.

(You get 1 mark for using a suitable format.)

Your writing style should:
- Be formal because you don't know the person you're writing to personally.
- Have a suitable formal greeting and sign-off.

(You get 1 mark for using a suitable tone and style for your audience.)

You should include this information:
- When the appointment should have been, on 24th July at 11:30 am and why you need to change the appointment. For example, you are on holiday that week, or you can't get time off work.
- A suggestion for when you would like the appointment to be. For example, the week after or on 1st August.
- An explanation of the problem you are having with your teeth. For example, toothache or bleeding gums.

Use a clear structure:
- Start by explaining the purpose of the email. You want to change the time of the appointment.
- Go on to explain what the problem is and suggest an alternative time.
- End with what you want them to do. For example, book another time and reply to confirm it.

(You can get up to 4 marks for including suitable content in a sensible order.)

You should use correct spelling, punctuation and grammar.
(You can get up to 4 marks for using correct spelling, punctuation and grammar.)

You should be aiming to get around seven marks and above to pass.

Exercise I (Page 102)

You should set out your article suitably:
- Write a heading to show what the article is about. For example, 'Charity Walk' or 'Sponsored Swim'.
- You could use subheadings to break up the text. Use the bullet points as a rough guide.
- Write 'By' and your name at the end of the article to show who has written it.
- Use paragraphs and full sentences. You should start a new paragraph for each point.

(You can get up to 2 marks for setting out your article in a suitable way.)

Your writing style should:
- Be formal because it is for the company newsletter and people in charge might read it.
- Be informative because you want to give people lots of information about the event.
- Be clear because you want everyone to understand what you did.

(You can get up to 3 marks for using a suitable tone and style for your audience.)

You should include this information:
- What the event was. Write down what you had to do and for how long. For example, you did a 12 km sponsored run.
- When, where and who did it. For example, it was last week and took place in the local town. Five people from work took part.
- Which charity you were raising money for. For example, 'Cancer Trust'.
- You could also explain why you chose that charity. For example, you have been helped by the charity in the past.

- You could also include any other information about the event. For example, what the weather was like, who came to support you and whether you'd do it again.

Use a clear structure:
- Start by describing what the event was and why you did it.
- Go on to describe where, when and who did it.
- End by saying how much money you have raised so far.

(You can get up to 9 marks for including suitable content in a sensible order.)

You should use correct spelling, punctuation and grammar.
(You can get up to 11 marks for using correct spelling, punctuation and grammar.)

You should be aiming to get around seventeen marks and above to pass.

Exercise J (Page 103)

You should set out your leaflet suitably:
- Use a heading to show what the leaflet is about. For example, 'New Music Festival'.
- You could split the leaflet into sections using subheadings.
- You could use bullet points or numbered lists to break up the text and make the details clear.

(You can get up to 2 marks for using a suitable format.)

Your writing style should:
- Be informative, so you should use clear language and make sure you include all the facts.
- Be persuasive so that you encourage local people to come.
- Be friendly because you don't want to put anyone off coming.
- Use short sentences to make your leaflet easy to understand.
- Be the same for all of your leaflet. For example, if you start writing in an informal style, don't write some parts in a formal style.

(You can get up to 3 marks for using a suitable tone and style for your audience.)

You should include this information:
- When the festival is. It's on 15th August.
- What's on offer at the festival. Write a list of all the acts and what type of music they play.

Answers to the Writing Questions

- Mention that the festival will have food and craft stalls as well as a children's tent.
- Reasons for people to come along and take part. For example, to have a good time with friends, to hear a range of different types of live music or to visit the craft stalls. It's suitable for families because there is a children's tent.

Use a clear structure:
- You should group similar information together and put the most important points first.
- Start by writing the purpose of the leaflet. It's to give information about the festival.
- Go on to give details about when the festival is, what's on offer and why people should come and take part.
- End with a reminder that people should come along.

(You can get up to 7 marks for including suitable content in a sensible order.)

You should use correct spelling, punctuation and grammar.
(You can get up to 8 marks for using correct spelling, punctuation and grammar.)

You should be aiming to get around fourteen marks and above to pass.

Exercise K (Page 104)

You should set your email out correctly:
- Write 'To' followed by workers@workplace.co.uk to show who the email is for.
- Underneath, write 'From' and then your email address.
- Write 'Subject' followed by a suitable subject. For example, 'Surprise party' or 'Gavin's birthday'.
- Start your email with a suitable greeting. For example, 'Hello all'.
- Sign-off your email suitably. For example, 'Hope to see you there' and your name.
- Use paragraphs and full sentences. You should start a new paragraph for each point.

(You get 1 mark for using a suitable format.)

Your writing style should:
- Be informal because you know your work friends personally.

- Have a suitable greeting and sign-off.
- Be friendly but don't use any slang or text speak.

(You get 1 mark for using a suitable tone and style for your audience.)

You should include this information:
- The details of the party. Carly has organised a surprise birthday party for Gavin.
- The party is at the Swan pub at 7.30 pm on Friday 18th October, and there is a fancy dress theme.
- Reasons for your work friends to come along. For example, there will be a DJ and a buffet.
- What you're going to wear. For example, a pirate outfit. Suggest what costumes your friends could wear, like a cowboy or an alien.

Use a clear structure:
- Start by explaining the purpose of your email. You're inviting them to Gavin's birthday party.
- Go on to give the details of the party, followed by some reasons why they should come.
- Say what you will wear and make some suggestions for other costumes.
- End with what you want your work friends to do. For example, reply as soon as possible.

(You can get up to 4 marks for including suitable content in a sensible order.)

You should use correct spelling, punctuation and grammar.
(You can get up to 4 marks for using correct spelling, punctuation and grammar.)

You should be aiming to get around seven marks and above to pass.

Exercise L (Page 105)

You should set your letter out correctly:
- Write your name and address at the top right-hand side of the page.
- Write the date underneath your address.
- Write the full address of the councillor on the left-hand side of the page:
Mr Bird,
45 Red Lane,
Southampton,
SO17 8YS

- Start with 'Dear Mr Bird' because you know his name from the leaflet. Don't write 'Dear James' as it's too personal. Don't write 'Dear Sir/Madam'.
- End the letter with 'Yours sincerely', because you know the person's name.
- Use paragraphs and full sentences.

(You can get up to 2 marks for using the correct format.)

Your writing style should:
- Be formal because you don't know the person you're writing to personally.
- Be persuasive because you want the council to fund more community projects.
- Have a suitable greeting and sign-off for a formal letter.

(You can get up to 2 marks for using a suitable tone and style for your audience.)

You should include this information:
- Why you think the council should fund more community projects. For example, council taxes have gone up so community projects deserve more funding, or community projects reduce crime in an area.
- Why you think community projects are important. For example, sports fields are a safe place for young people to spend their free time, sports fields encourage people to keep fit, or parks make towns nicer.

Use a clear structure.
- Start with the purpose of the letter. You want to persuade him to fund more community projects.
- Go on to say why you think they should fund more projects.
- End with what you think the council should do. For example, give more money to local sports facilities or reopen parks that have closed.

(You can get up to 5 marks for including suitable content in a sensible order.)

You should use correct spelling, punctuation and grammar.
(You can get up to 6 marks for using correct spelling, punctuation and grammar.)

You should be aiming to get around ten marks and above to pass.

Glossary

A

Advert

A text that persuades the reader to do something. For example, buy a product or visit an attraction.

Apostrophe

A punctuation mark that shows missing letters in a word or that something belongs to someone.

Article

A text from a newspaper or magazine.

Audience

The person or people who read a text.

B

Bullet points

A way of breaking up information into separate points in a list.

C

Caption

Text that tells you more about a graphic.

Comma

A punctuation mark that is used to separate different items in a list.

Controlled assessment

A part of the qualification that is taken during class time and marked by the teacher.

D

Descriptive writing

Writing that tells the reader what something is like in detail.

E

Email

An electronic message sent from one computer to another.

F

Font

How letters look when they are typed. For example, **bold** or *italics*.

Formal writing

A type of writing that sounds serious and professional.

Format

How texts are laid out on a page.

G

Glossary

A part of a text which explains the meaning of difficult words.

Graphic

A picture, diagram or chart.

I

Impersonal writing

Writing that doesn't tell you anything about the writer's personality or opinions.

Informal writing

Writing that sounds chatty and friendly.

Informative writing

Writing that tells the reader about something. It usually uses a lot of facts.

Instructive writing

Writing that tells the reader how to do something.

Glossary

Layout
How a text is presented on the page using different presentational features.

Leaflet
A text, which is usually given away for free, that tells the reader about something.

Letter
A text written to a person, or a group of people, which is sent in the post.

Personal writing
Writing that is written from the writer's point of view. It is full of opinions and emotions. It sounds like it's talking to the reader.

Persuasive writing
Writing that tries to convince the reader to do or feel something.

Prefixes
Letters added to the start of a word which change the word's meaning.

Presentational features
Any part of the text which affects the layout. For example, headings, graphics or captions.

Purpose
The reason a text is written.

References
A part of a text which tells the reader where the writer got their information from.

Report
A text that gives the reader information about something that has happened or might happen.

Shortened word
A word which is shortened with an apostrophe. For example, 'didn't' or 'hasn't'.

Silent letters
Letters in a word which you can't hear when the word is said aloud, for example the 'b' in lamb.

Style
The way a text is written. For example, formal or informal.

Suffixes
Letters added to the end of a word which change the word's meaning.

Tense
Whether a verb is talking about an action in the past, present or future.

Text type
The kind of text, for example an advert or report.

Tone
The way a text sounds to the reader. For example, personal or impersonal.

Verb
A doing or being word.

Webpage
A type of text found on a website.

Index

Index